Level 4

by Marie Rippel

All rights reserved. No portion of this publication may be reproduced by any means, including duplicating, photocopying, electronic, mechanical, recording, the World Wide Web, e-mail, or otherwise, without written permission from the publisher.

Copyright © 2015, 2011 by All About® Learning Press, Inc.
Printed in the United States of America

All About® Learning Press, Inc.
615 Commerce Loop
Eagle River, WI 54521

ISBN 978-1-935197-02-7
v. 1.2.0

Editor: Renée LaTulippe
Layout and Cover Design: Dave LaTulippe

The *All About® Spelling* Level 4 Teacher's Manual is part of the *All About® Spelling* program.

For more books in this series, go to www.AllAboutSpelling.com.

Contents

1 Preparing for Level 4
Gather the Materials 3
Set Up the Spelling Review Box 4
Familiarize Yourself with the New Phonograms 5
Organize the Letter Tiles 6
Learn How to Handle Troublemakers 8
Learn About Spelling Strategies 10
Discover What's New in Level 4 11

2 Complete Step-by-Step Lesson Plans
Step 1: Warming Up 15
Step 2: Consonant Team TCH 21
Step 3: Consonant Team DGE 27
Step 4: Ways to Spell /j/ 33
Step 5: Prefixes 35
Step 6: The Four Sounds of Y 39
Step 7: The /er/ of *Works* 45
Step 8: Months of the Year 51
Step 9: The Sound of /oo/ Spelled EW 57
Step 10: Short E Spelled EA 63
Step 11: Ways to Spell /ĕ/ 67
Step 12: The Sound of /r/ Spelled WR 71
Step 13: The Sound of /n/ Spelled KN 75
Step 14: More ER Words 79
Step 15: The Sound of /ŭ/ Spelled O 83
Step 16: Practice Spelling Strategies 87
Step 17: Words with EIGH and Numbers 91
Step 18: The Sounds of /ū/ and /oo/ Spelled UE 97
Step 19: PH and the /er/ of *Early* 101
Step 20: Unaccented A 105
Step 21: Long A Spelled EA 109
Step 22: /shŭn/ Spelled TION 113
Step 23: Ways to Spell /er/ 117
Step 24: /wōr/ Spelled WAR 121
Step 25: The Sound of /ē/ Spelled EY 125
Step 26: The Sound of /ō/ Spelled OE 139
Step 27: The /ĭk/ Words 133

3 Appendices
Appendix A: Phonograms Taught in Level 4 139
Appendix B: Scope and Sequence of Level 4 141
Appendix C: The Jobs of Silent E 143
Appendix D: The Six Syllable Types 145
Appendix E: Words Taught in Level 4 147

1
Preparing for Level 4

Gather the Materials

Following is the list of materials you will need for teaching Level 4:

- ☐ Student Packet for Level 4
- ☐ Set of *All About Spelling* Letter Tiles
- ☐ Spelling review box or index card box
- ☐ Yellow colored pencil
- ☐ Lined notebook paper

You will also need these items from your student's Level 3 Spelling Review Box:

- ☐ Phonogram Cards 1-53
- ☐ Sound Cards 1-59
- ☐ Key Cards 1-19

The following items are optional:

- ☐ Stickers or colored pencils for the Progress Chart
- ☐ *Phonogram Sounds* app (recommended)
- ☐ Letter tile magnets
- ☐ 2' x 3' Magnetic white board
- ☐ Silent E Book (from Level 3 or available separately)
- ☐ Calendar (used in Steps 8 and 18)

Set Up the Spelling Review Box

The continual, individualized review featured in *All About Spelling* ensures that your students don't forget what you teach them and that they get the practice they need in exactly the areas they need it. Flashcards help accomplish much of this review, and the Spelling Review Box keeps them all organized.

As in previous levels, four types of flashcards will be used:

These yellow cards offer **visual and verbal review**: you hold up the card and your student says the sound(s) the phonogram makes. You have 53 Phonogram Cards from previous levels, and 12 new Phonogram Cards are included with Level 4.

Each red flashcard offers **aural and tactile review**: you dictate the sound and your student listens and writes the letter(s) that make the sound. You have 59 Sound Cards from previous levels, and 16 new Sound Cards are included with Level 4.

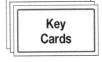
Each blue flashcard contains a rule or generalization about spelling. They are used during lessons to **reinforce new concepts**. You read and review these flashcards with your student. Your student's Spelling Review Box should contain Key Cards 1-19 from previous levels plus the 3 new cards included with Level 4.

Each green flashcard contains a word that students learn to spell in Level 4. These cards offer **aural, verbal, and tactile review**: you dictate the word and your student writes the word.

Follow these steps to set up the Spelling Review Box:

1. Place the laminated divider cards (located in your Interactive Kit) in the Spelling Review Box in numerical order.

2. Separate the new Phonogram Cards, Sound Cards, Key Cards, and Word Cards. Put all flashcards behind the appropriate Future Lessons dividers.

3. Transfer all Phonogram Cards, Sound Cards, and Key Cards from Level 3 into the Level 4 Spelling Review Box. Place them behind the appropriate Mastered dividers. These cards will continue to be reviewed to keep the concepts fresh in your student's mind.

Familiarize Yourself with the New Phonograms

In Level 4, twelve new phonograms will be taught through hands-on work with the letter tiles and review with the flashcards. Your student will learn to hear the individual sounds in words and how to represent those sounds with the phonograms.

Download the *Phonogram Sounds* app. This free program for your computer, tablet, or phone features clear pronunciation of the sounds of all 72 basic phonograms (letters and letter combinations). Download the app at www.allaboutlearningpress.com/phonogram-sounds-app or scan the QR code. *(Note: If you'd prefer not to download the app, a CD-ROM version is available for purchase.)*

Practice saying the sound(s) before teaching them in the lesson. This way, you will be able to model the sounds of the phonograms accurately for your students. You won't have to wonder if you are pronouncing them correctly—you will know for sure!

You will see a key word printed on the back of each Phonogram Card. The key word is there to help trigger your memory when you are working with your student. With the exception of the phonograms that spell /er/, do not teach the key word to your student. It is there for your use as the teacher, not for the student to memorize. We want the student to make an instant connection between seeing the phonogram and saying the sound. Requiring key words such as "/n/ as in *knee*" or illustrating the phonograms with pictures will slow down the formation of that connection.

The following phonograms are taught in Level 4:

tch	**dge**	**ew**
ei	**wr**	**kn**
eigh	**ear**	**ph**
ti	**oe**	

Generalizations and rules are taught to help the student choose the correct phonogram to represent the sound.

Organize the Letter Tiles

We will continue to use the specially color-coded letter tiles to teach new spelling concepts.

Organize the letter tiles as follows in preparation for teaching Level 4:

1. Cut apart the letter tiles and labels.
2. Label three plastic baggies **Use Now**, **Use Later**, and **Save for Level 5**. Sort the letter tiles and labels into the appropriate bags, as shown below.

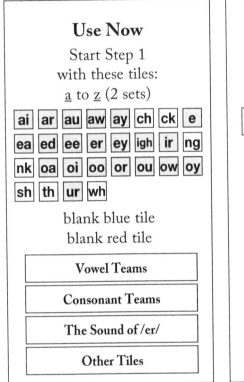
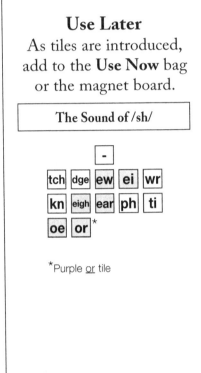

Consider using a magnetic white board during the spelling lessons.

Most teachers magnetize the letter tiles and store them on a magnetic white board. This is a great way to keep the tiles organized between lessons and to save time, too. If you opt to go this route, the following tips for preparing and using the letter tiles on a magnetic white board will help get you started.

- If you purchased the precut magnetic strips from *All About Spelling*, simply peel off the paper backing and center one magnet on the back of each letter tile and two magnets on the back of each heading label. (The heading labels are the longer tiles with names such as "Consonant Teams," "Vowel Teams," and "The Sound of /er/.")

- The magnetic white board should be a minimum of 2' high x 3' wide. That will give you enough room for the full set of letters, plus plenty of open space to work in. You can go larger, of course, but it's not necessary.

- Before purchasing a board, check the product description to be sure it's actually magnetic. Boards may go by several names—magnet board, magnetic board, dry erase board, white board, marker board—but magnets will not necessarily stick to all of them. Consider purchasing a board with a dry erase feature, which is a nice addition to your daily lessons that offers yet another tactile way for your students to practice their spelling words.
- You can work with the tiles right on the magnet board, or remove just the tiles you need for the lesson and arrange them on the table.

Whether you work on the table or on a magnetic white board, the letter tiles should be set up in the same arrangement for each lesson. This will enable you and your student to quickly locate the tiles you need. To give you the big picture, here is the tile layout after all the phonograms have been introduced:

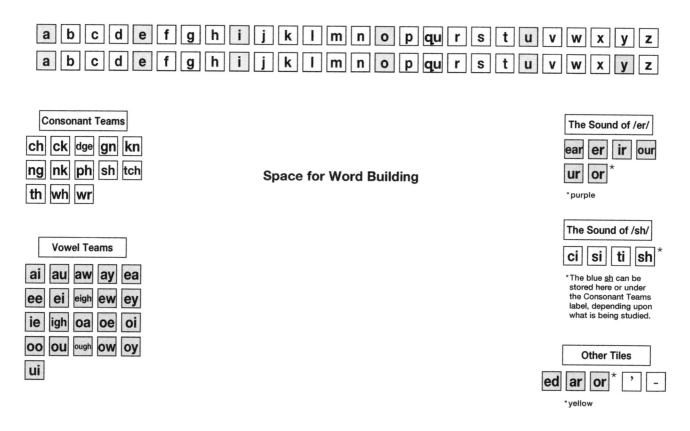

The initial letter tile setup is shown in Step 1 on page 15. Only letter tiles that have been introduced in the lessons should be displayed. Store the rest in the plastic baggies.

While most students enjoy using manipulatives, there are always those who do not. If your student does not like using the letter tiles, you can easily adapt the lesson plans. Whenever a concept is illustrated with the letter tiles, simply write out the words on a dry erase board or on paper instead.

Learn How to Handle Troublemakers

The vast majority of words in the English language follow the rules and generalizations taught on the Key Cards. However, there are always the Troublemakers—those words that, for one reason or another, are challenging to spell.

To tame these Troublemakers, you need to figure out why the student is misspelling the word and then apply the correct remedy. The following list outlines four common reasons for misspelling a word and provides specific strategies for correcting the problem.

Reason #1: The student misspells a word you think he should be able to spell. For example, your student writes down the word *form* instead of *from*, and you know that he has spelled this word correctly on other occasions.

>**Strategy:** Ask the student to slowly read exactly what he wrote down, making sure that he reads each phonogram. The student will often catch and correct his own mistake. If he doesn't, tell him, "You wrote *form*, but we want the word *from*. What do you need to change?"

Reason #2: The student's pronunciation of a word makes it difficult to spell. If a student learns to pronounce a word clearly, he will usually be able to spell it correctly. Some words that are commonly mispronounced and misspelled are *probably (probly)*, *secretary (secertary)*, *because (becuz)*, and *library (libary)*. Other words are not pronounced clearly in everyday speech. For example, most Americans pronounce the word *button* as *butn* and *little* as *liddle*. The vowel sound in the unaccented syllable gets lost in the normal rhythm of speech. Regional accents can also make certain words more challenging.

>**Strategy:** Model the correct pronunciation of the word and have your student repeat and segment the word syllable by syllable. In the case of unaccented syllables or regional accents, have the student "pronounce for spelling," enunciating each syllable clearly and as it is written. This technique was introduced in Level 1 and will be used throughout the series.

Reason #3: The student forgot a rule or generalization.

>**Strategy:** Pull out the related Key Card and review the concept. Demonstrate the rule by using the letter tiles to spell the troublesome word. Keep the Key Card behind the Review divider for daily practice until your student demonstrates mastery of that concept.

Reason #4: The misspelled word is a Rule Breaker. A Rule Breaker is a word that does not follow the rules of spelling. For example, in the word *said* we expect the ai to say /ā/, not /ĕ/.

>**Strategy:** Using the Word Card, have the student identify the tricky part of the offending word, circle the letters that don't say what we expect them to say, and color in the circle to highlight the problem. Then have him write the word on paper.

If your student continues to misspell the same Troublemakers, try one of these additional strategies:

>**Writing Intensive.** In the writing intensive exercise, the student looks at the troublesome word and then looks at an empty spot on the table. He pictures the word on the table and spells the word aloud three times. Then with his finger, he writes the word in VERY BIG LETTERS on the table three times. Finally, he spells the word on paper three times. In the space of a minute, the student has practiced the word nine times.

Tactile Practice. In this exercise, your student "writes" the Troublemaker on a tactile surface, using his pointer finger instead of a pencil. Some surfaces to consider include:
- Sand in a shoe box lid
- A sheet of fine sandpaper
- "Feely" fabrics such as burlap, velvet, or corduroy
- Rice poured into a baking pan
- Plush carpet square

The following items can be put into a sealed plastic baggie to create a no-mess surface. Your student can then use his finger to write through the bag.
- Shaving cream
- Pudding (This one you can eat after the lesson!)
- Liquid soap
- Glue

Two ways to burn something into memory are frequency (repeated review) and intensity (different and surprising treatment), so keep that in mind as you handle the Troublemakers.

Learn About Spelling Strategies

All About Spelling approaches spelling as a thinking subject, not merely as a subject for memorization. Spelling strategies give students another tool to help them move to a higher level of spelling ability. Such strategies especially benefit students with dyslexia and other learning differences.

Good spellers use different strategies for different words. Some words call for more than one strategy. In Level 4, students will learn to ask themselves, "What strategy will help me spell this word?"

Following are the spelling strategies emphasized in Level 4:

1. Pronounce for Spelling

Students have already used this technique in previous levels, but we will expand on it in Level 4. Students will learn to emphasize the unaccented syllable in a word so that they can hear the vowel sound more clearly. For example, when they learn to spell the word *important*, they will first pronounce it /im-por-TANT/, emphasizing the syllable /TANT/ so they can hear the /ă/ sound.

2. Analyze the Word

In Level 3, your student learned to analyze words under your direction. In Level 4, we take this to the next level by encouraging students to ask themselves questions when they encounter an unfamiliar spelling word.
- Which letters are used to spell each sound?
- Are there any spelling rules that apply?
- How many syllables are there?
- If there is a Silent E, what is its job?
- Is there a suffix or prefix?

3. Scratch Paper Spelling

There is often more than one way to spell a sound, especially when it comes to vowel sounds. The student may be faced with a dilemma: is *neat* spelled "neet" or "neat"? Scratch paper spelling is the technique of trying out different potential spellings of a word to see what "looks right." This technique encourages students to try out various spelling options and helps them recognize and select the correct one.

4. Identify the Base Word

Recognizing the base word will often give students a clue to spelling a multisyllable word. When faced with the word *knowledge*, for example, the student can first locate the base word *know*. Breaking down the word into its components helps the student spell the longer word.

Discover What's New in Level 4

Now it's time to take a look at the other materials that are included in the Student Packet. Some will look familiar, like the Word Banks, Syllable Division Rules Chart, and Homophones List. Level 4 also includes some new tools to help you present the lessons clearly and to help your student learn through verbal, visual, and tactile means.

For now, you may wish to store the remaining items in a large manila envelope. This way, when they are called for in the "You will need" section of a Step, you will know right where to find them. Complete instructions for their use will be provided in the lesson plans.

If you are curious about the new materials, here is a sneak peek:

 **New Materials and Activities**

In Level 4 you will find several new activities and tools that will help your student internalize new concepts. Look for the **New!** flag for tips on how to use the materials and for additional information on activities.

| Spelling Strategies Chart | The **Spelling Strategies Chart** summarizes strategies the student learns in Level 4 to help him become a strong speller. |

 The **Spotlight on Silent E** is a quick activity that reinforces and builds upon your student's understanding of the jobs of Silent E.

Prefix Tiles — In addition to the letter tiles, your student will be using prefix tiles to build words. The prefix tiles offer **visual and tactile** practice for the student to help him recognize and correctly use prefixes.

2
Complete Step-by-Step Lesson Plans

Following are twenty-seven Steps. Each Step contains a major concept that needs to be mastered by the student in order to form a strong foundation for spelling. Each Step should be mastered before moving on to the next Step. Schedule as many (or as few!) study sessions as your student needs in order to understand the concept in each Step.

Step 1 - Warming Up

This is a fast-paced review of concepts taught in previous levels. Your student will also learn the tch and dge phonograms.

You will need: Phonogram Cards 1-55, Sound Cards 1-61, Key Cards 1-19, Spelling Strategies Chart, Syllable Division Rules Chart, letter tiles tch and dge, stickers or colored pencils, progress chart

For each lesson, arrange the letter tiles as shown below, adding new tiles when indicated.

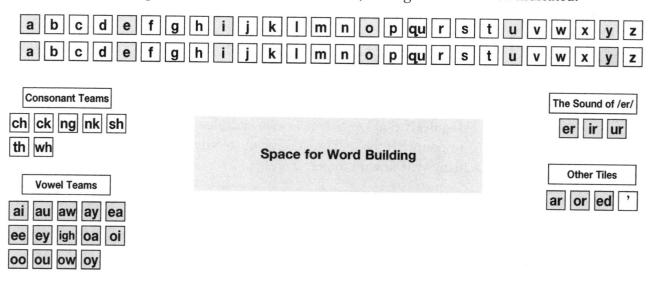

Review

Review Phonogram Cards 1-53

Do a brisk review of Phonogram Cards 1-53 from the previous levels. Hold up each card and have your student say the sound(s) of the phonogram. Place the cards that your student has mastered behind the Mastered divider. Cards that your student should review again go behind the Review divider.

Review Sound Cards 1-59

Review Sound Cards 1-59 from the previous levels. Dictate the sound(s) and have your student write the letter or letter combination that makes the sound(s). He should say the sound as he writes the phonogram. Sort behind the Mastered and Review dividers.

Step 1: Warming Up

Review
(continued)

Review Key Cards 1-19

Review Key Cards 1-19 from the previous levels. Read the front of each card and have your student provide the response on the back. If necessary, use the letter tiles to demonstrate spelling rules or generalizations your student may need help with. File the cards behind the appropriate Mastered and Review dividers.

> **New!** Throughout Level 4, your student will be learning spelling strategies designed to help him become a strong speller.

Discuss Spelling Strategy #1

Take out the Spelling Strategies Chart. Cover the chart with a blank piece of paper.

"Good spellers use different strategies for different words. You already know some good spelling strategies. Today we are going to talk about some of them."

"The first one is **Pronounce for Spelling**."

"Say we want to spell the word *interest*. Normally, we say the word so quickly that we only hear two syllables. But if we slow down and pronounce it for spelling, the word sounds like this: *in–ter–est*. How many syllables are there?" *Three.*

"Right. And when we can hear all three syllables, we can spell the word syllable by syllable."

Using the letter tiles, demonstrate spelling the word one syllable at a time.

Uncover Strategy #1 on the chart. "So our first strategy is: Pronounce for Spelling."

Discuss Spelling Strategy #2

"The second strategy you can use is **Analyze the Word**. In the last level, we did Word Analysis at the beginning of each lesson. That is where we look at a word, like *gentleness*, and analyze the different parts of it." Build the word *gentleness*.

"Let's analyze this word right now."

"What letter is making the /j/ sound?" *G*.

Step 1: Warming Up

Review
(continued)

"Why is the g soft?" *Because of the e.*

"Is there a suffix?" *Yes.*

Move the suffix into its own syllable." *Student divides the word.*

"What is the job of Silent E here?" *To add a vowel to the second syllable.*

"Good. So you located the suffix, the base word, and the job of Silent E. Looking at new words in this way will help you become a better speller."

Uncover Strategy #2 on the chart. "This is our second strategy: Analyze the Word."

"You can use these strategies on your own when you come across a word you don't already know how to spell. Later in this book, we will discuss more spelling strategies, too."

Review Syllable Division Rules and Syllable Types

Take out the Syllable Division Rules Chart. Cover Rule #5 because it has not yet been taught. Read through Rules #1-4 with your student.

Build the following words. Have your student divide them into syllables and label the syllable types.

> For your reference as teacher, the six syllable types are listed in Appendix D.
>
> The six syllable types were covered extensively in previous levels. If you feel that your student needs additional practice in this area, choose several words per lesson and have your student label the syllables.

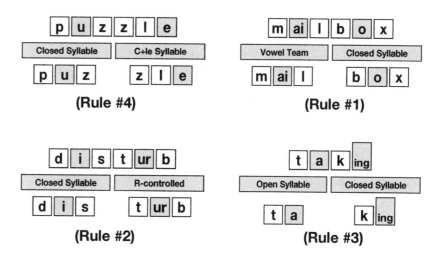

Step 1: Warming Up

Review
(continued)

Review Suffix Rules

"You learned three rules for adding suffixes in Level 3. Let's review them."

The 1-1-1 Rule

Does the word have:
 1 syllable?
 1 vowel?
 1 consonant at the end?

If the answer to every question is YES, then double the last letter before adding a vowel suffix.

(Key Card 14)

"Change *swim* to *swimmer*." Student doubles the m and adds suffix er.

"Why did you double the m?" *Because of the 1-1-1 Rule (or, because it would spell* swimer *if you didn't double the m. We have to protect the short vowel).*

"Change *fast* to *faster*." Student adds suffix er.

"Why didn't you double the t?" *It didn't have just one consonant at the end (or, the vowel was already protected by the s).*

"Read this word." *Joked.*

"What is the last sound you hear in the word *joked*?" */t/.*

"How is the /t/ sound spelled?" *Ed.*

"What is the base word of the word *joked*?" *Joke.*

Drop the E Rule

Use the Drop the E Rule when you add a vowel suffix.

(Key Card 18)

"Change *make* to *making*." Student drops the e and adds suffix ing.

Change the Y to I Rule

If a word ends in a single vowel y, change the y to an i and add the suffix (unless the suffix begins with an i).

(Key Card 19)

"Read this word." *Copy.*

"What is the sound of the letter y in this word?" */ē/.*

"Is the y a vowel or a consonant here?" *Vowel.*

"Change this word to *copier*." Student changes the y to an i and adds suffix er.

Build the word *copy* again. "Now change the word to *copying*." Student adds suffix ing.

"Why didn't you change the y to an i?" *Because the suffix begins with an i, and we don't put two i's together.*

Step 1: Warming Up

New Teaching   **Teach New Phonograms TCH and DGE**

"We have two new tiles today."

Point to the tch tile. |tch|

"This tile says **/ch/, three-letter /ch/**. Repeat after me: /ch/, three-letter /ch/." *Student repeats.*

Point to the dge tile. |dge|

"This tile says **/j/, three-letter /j/**. Repeat after me: /j/, three-letter /j/." *Student repeats.*

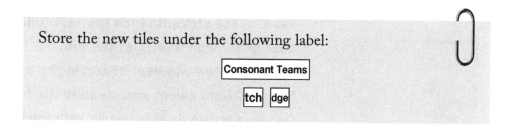

Take out Phonogram Cards 54 and 55 and practice them with your student.

Practice Sound Cards 60 and 61 with your student. Dictate the sound and have your student write the phonogram.

File the cards behind the appropriate Review dividers in the Spelling Review Box.

Step 1: Warming Up

Reinforcement

Say the sentence only once! Your student should repeat the sentence before he begins to write. By saying the words out loud, he will remember them more easily and be able to write them down accurately.

Dictate Sentences

Dictate several sentences each day. The sentences for this review lesson contain words that were taught in Levels 1, 2, and 3.

Ted has thirty warm black coats.
Don't forget to feed the pigs.
Dad told Tom to paint the house red.
Are you swimming in that muddy water?
My lazy cat is taking a nap on the lawn.
The toothless tiger hid in the grass.
I enjoy all the flowers and birds in April.
Will they play those loud trumpets tonight?
None of the students took the test today.
Your sister won a prize at the fair.
We live on the windiest hilltop in the city.
Ken and Beth swept and cleaned the boat.
Do you want to do this puzzle with me?
That's a very ugly purple skirt!
Who is the fastest runner in school?
Pam pushed the box of junk under the bed.
Seven ships were lost on the foggy sea.
The small stick sank in the quicksand.
Rick is quite cheerful in the morning.
It was a dark and stormy night.

Mark the Progress Chart

After each lesson has been mastered, have your student color in or place a sticker over that Step number on the chart.

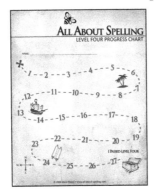

Step 2 - Consonant Team TCH

This lesson will teach how to choose between ch and tch to spell the sound of /ch/ and how to spell words containing tch.

You will need: Key Card 20, Sound Card 62, Word Cards 1-10

Review

New Teaching

Teach Key Card 20: Use TCH after a Short Vowel

"Here are two ways to spell the sound of /ch/."

Pull down tiles <u>ch</u> and <u>tch</u>.

Build the word *match*, placing a blank blue tile in place of the /ch/ sound.

"I want to spell the word *match*. In place of this blank tile, I need to decide whether to use the <u>ch</u> or the <u>tch</u>."

"Is this a short vowel?" *Yes.*

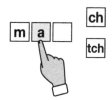

"It is, so we use <u>tch</u>."

Replace the blank tile with the <u>tch</u> tile.

New Teaching
(continued)

"Let's try another word. The word I want to spell is *porch*."

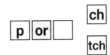

"I need to decide whether to use the ch or the tch."

Point to the or tile. "Is this a short vowel?" *No.*

"Or is not a short vowel, so we use ch."

"We **usually** use tch when the sound of /ch/ comes **right after** a short vowel."

> When deciding whether to use the tch or the ch, be sure to look **only** to the letter IMMEDIATELY preceding the /ch/ sound. There may be a short vowel elsewhere in the word, but we are only concerned with the letter that comes directly before the /ch/ sound.

Have your student practice this concept with the following words. Build the word for your student, putting a blank blue tile in place of the /ch/ sound.

ranch　　**stitch**　　**patch**　　**speech**　　**itch**

Read Key Card 20 with your student and then file it behind the Review divider.

> There are a few exceptions to this generalization: *rich, such,* and *much* (all taught in Level 1), *which* (taught in Level 2), and *attach, detach, bachelor,* and *duchess.*

New Teaching
(continued)

Teach Sound Card 62

"Today we have a new Sound Card."

Read Sound Card 62:

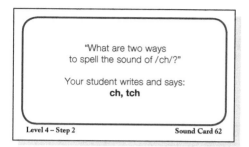

Practice this Sound Card with your student and then store it behind the Review divider.

These "summary" Sound Cards were introduced in Level 3 and will continue to be used in Level 4. Remind your student that he should say the name of the letters as he writes them down.

Word Cards 1-10: Spell on Paper

Dictate the words and have your student spell them on paper. The student should write one word per line.

1. inch
2. catch
3. branch
4. stitch
5. ranch
6. match
7. lunch
8. kitchen
9. itch
10. speech

File the Word Cards behind the Review divider.

Step 2: Consonant Team TCH

Reinforcement **More Words**

The following words reinforce the concepts taught in Step 2. Have your student spell them for additional practice.

bench	bunch	crunch	ditch	fetch
patch	porch	switch	stretch	sketch
scratch	French	pinch	punch	munch

Dictate Sentences

Dictate several sentences each day.

Put the dishes in the kitchen.
The French girl ate lunch on the porch.
I have an itch on my foot.
Beth gave a speech to the class.
A bunch of flowers grows in the ditch.
Don't pinch me!
I sat on the bench at the game.
Did the cat scratch your hand?
Bob made a sketch of our ranch.
I want to munch on some popcorn!
A branch of the tree fell down.
Uncle Ted plays fetch with his dog.

Reinforcement
(continued)

Writing Station

Dictate each word and have your student write it on paper. Then have your student write original sentences using the new words.

loudly   **brownish**

scratching   **hear** (hear a sound)

begging

The Writing Station gives your student the opportunity to use his spelling skills. You will note that the words are related for added interest.

There are two types of words included in the Writing Station:

1. **Words containing suffixes (and later, prefixes).** Your student already knows the base words, but must use his knowledge of adding suffixes to properly spell the words.

2. **Homophones.** This will give your student practice in correct usage.

Step 3 - Consonant Team DGE

This lesson will teach how to choose between g and dge to spell the sound of /j/ at the end of a word.

You will need: Key Card 21, Silent E Book (optional), Word Cards 11-20, Homophones List

Review

New Teaching   **Teach Key Card 21: Use DGE after a Short Vowel**

"Pull down three ways to spell the sound of /j/." *Student pulls down j, g, and dge.*

| j | g | dge |

"Today we are going to talk about the sound of /j/ at the **end of a word**. One of these tiles can't be used at the **end** of English words. Which one is that?" *The j.*

"Right. Set that tile aside." *Student sets the j tile aside.*

Place an <u>e</u> tile next to the g. | g | e | | dge |

At the **end of a word**, we have two ways to spell the sound of /j/: g followed by Silent E, and <u>dge</u>."

Build the word *fudge*, placing a blank tile in place of the /j/ sound.

| f | u | □ |

"I want to spell the word *fudge*. In place of this blank tile, I need to decide whether to use the g-e or the <u>dge</u>."

"Is this a short vowel?" *Yes.*

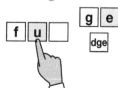

"It is, so we use <u>dge</u>."

Replace the blank tile with the <u>dge</u> tile.

| f | u | dge |

Step 3: Consonant Team DGE

New Teaching
(continued)

"Let's try another word. The word I want to spell is *charge*."

"I need to decide whether to use the g-e or the dge."

Point to the ar tile. "Is this a short vowel?" *No.*

"Ar is not a short vowel, so we use g-e."

"We only use dge **right after** a short vowel."

> When deciding whether to use g-e or dge at the end of a word, be sure to look **only** to the letter IMMEDIATELY preceding the /j/ sound. There may be a short vowel elsewhere in the word, but we are only concerned with the letter that comes directly before the /j/ sound.

Have your student practice this concept with the following words. Build the word for your student, putting a blank blue tile in place of the /j/ sound.

bridge   **rage**   **ledge**   **large**   **judge**

Read Key Card 21 with your student and place behind the Review divider.

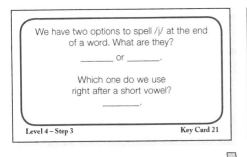
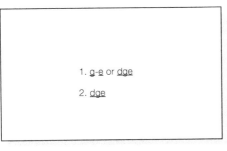

> Take a look at the dge phonogram in the word *bridge* (or any dge word). The d acts as a "buffer" so Silent E doesn't make the vowel long. The d protects the vowel from Silent E.

Step 3: Consonant Team DGE

New Teaching
(continued)

Spotlight on Silent E

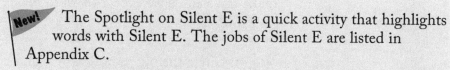

The Spotlight on Silent E is a quick activity that highlights words with Silent E. The jobs of Silent E are listed in Appendix C.

Your student can refer to his Silent E Book from Level 3. If you like, he can also add new spelling words to the book.

Build the word *judge*. | j | u | dge |

"The word *judge* ends in Silent E. What is the job of Silent E in this word?" *It makes the g soft (or, it makes the g say /j/).*

Teach Three Rule Breakers

"Three words on today's word list are Rule Breakers."

Build the word *could*. | c | ou | l | d |

"This word is *could*. Which letters don't say the sounds we expect them to say?" Lead your student to see that the ou sounds like /o͝o/ and the l is silent.

Show Word Card 18 to your student.

"Circle the <u>oul</u> in this word because those letters don't make the sounds we expect them to make." *Student circles the letters and fills in the circle with yellow pencil.*

"Spell the word *could* on paper." *Student writes the word.*

Step 3: Consonant Team DGE

New Teaching
(continued)

Take out Word Cards 19 and 20. "The words *would* and *should* are similar to the word *could* and are also Rule Breakers. Which letters don't make the sounds we expect them to make?" *The ou sounds like /o͝o/ and the l is silent.*

"Right. Circle the <u>ou</u>l in both words and color them yellow."

"Spell the word *would* on paper." *Student writes the word.*

"Spell the word *should* on paper." *Student writes the word.*

Have your student practice these three words until they become easy.

If your student has a tough time with these words, try the following strategies:

1. Teach *could* first. Once your student has mastered that word, the others will come easily.

2. Try saying a "cheer" to help your student get the rhythm and spelling of these words: **<u>C</u>** (pause), **<u>O</u>** (pause), **<u>U</u>-<u>L</u>-<u>D</u>** (said quickly together).

3. Though the jail routine won't be included in the Level 4 lesson plans, by all means continue to use it if you think your student will benefit from and enjoy it.

New Teaching
(continued)

Word Cards 11-20: Spell on Paper

Dictate the words and have your student spell them on paper.

11. edge
12. bridge
13. judge
14. charge
15. fudge
16. ridge
17. rage
18. could
19. would   Would you like some milk?
20. should

> **Tip!** If a spelling word has a homophone—another word that sounds alike but is spelled differently—use the word in a sentence. The student does not write the sentence.

File the Word Cards behind the Review divider.

Reinforcement

More Words

The following words reinforce the concepts taught in Step 3. Have your student spell them for additional practice.

badge   **ledge**   **hedge**

Homophone Pairs

New! The Homophone Pairs activity appears whenever a lesson introduces a new word that forms a homophone pair with another word that the student has already learned.

In this case, the student learned the word *wood* in Level 3, which can now be paired with the new spelling word *would*.

Have your student add the following homophone pair to the Homophones List. Students can start a new list for Level 4 or continue the same list started in Level 3.

would / wood

Read the following sentences and have your student point to the correct word on the Homophones List.

Would you help me?
The baseball bat is made of wood.
I would never say that!
Bring me wood for the fire.

Step 3: Consonant Team DGE

Reinforcement
(continued)

Dictate Sentences

Dictate several sentences each day.

> Should we take the bus?
> Don't stand on the edge of the cliff!
> The judge said I was the best swimmer!
> Could you speak louder?
> There is a green hedge in front of my house.
> We ran over the high bridge.
> I have a red badge on my shirt.
> The plant is on the window ledge.
> I wish Mom would make us some fudge!
> What can you see from the ridge of the hill?
> That man is in a rage!
> I had to pay a charge to cross the road.

Writing Station

Dictate each word and have your student write it on paper. Then have your student write original sentences using the new words.

sickness	**weak** (weak arms)
itches	**some** (some cats)
catching	

You can use the Writing Station as a diagnostic tool. Is your student misspelling any words when he creates his own sentences? Take a look at the types of errors he makes to determine if you need to review or reteach any concepts.

Step 4 - Ways to Spell /j/

In this lesson, your student will analyze three ways to spell the sound of /j/.

You will need: Sound Card 63

Review

New Teaching **Introduce the Word Sort for /j/**

Write these three headings across the top of lined paper. Draw vertical lines to form three columns:

j	g	dge

Point to the column headings. "Here are three ways to spell the sound of /j/."

Give your student a new sheet of lined paper. "I will dictate a word, and you will write it down on your paper. When you are satisfied that you have spelled the word correctly, copy the word to the correct column on this chart."

Dictate the following words:

gentle	**joyful**	**jumping**
ledge	**joking**	**stage**
bridge	**large**	**rage**
badge		

Step 4: Ways to Spell /j/

New Teaching
(continued)

Teach Sound Card 63

"Today we have a new Sound Card."

Read Sound Card 63:

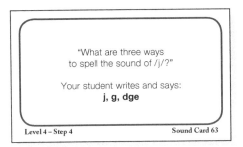

Practice this Sound Card with your student and then store it behind the Review divider.

Dictate Sentences

Dictate several sentences each day.

That patch of grass is too dry.
We will chop wood today.
He made one stitch with the needle.
I hear the twigs crunch under my feet.
Did he punch you in the arm?
Stretch your legs a little.
Pam lights the fire with a match.
Amy rides her bike on hilly paths.
Stop scratching those bug bites!
Would you switch places with me?
I think I'm catching a cold.
My nose itches!

There are no new Word Cards for Step 4.

Writing Station

Dictate each word and have your student write it on paper. Then have your student write original sentences using the new words.

chopping   **hikes**
lighting   **wood** (made of wood)
branches

Step 4: Ways to Spell /j/

Step 5 - Prefixes

In this lesson, your student will learn four new phonograms and how to spell words containing prefixes.

You will need: letter tiles ew, ei, wr, and kn, Phonogram Cards 56-59, Sound Cards 64-67, Key Card 22, prefix tiles

Review

New Teaching   **Teach New Phonograms EW, EI, WR, and KN**

"We have four new tiles today."

Point to the ew tile.   `ew`

"This tile says /ōō/–/ū/. Repeat after me: /ōō/–/ū/." *Student repeats.*

Point to the ei tile.   `ei`

"This tile says /ā/–/ē/ **that we may <u>not</u> use at the end of English words**. Repeat after me: /ā/–/ē/ that we may **not** use at the end of English words." *Student repeats.*

> Phonogram ei will be used in only one word in Level 4: the high-frequency word *their* in Step 9.
>
> The relatively few words that use ei include *either, ceiling, receive, veil, heir, reign, beige, foreign, forfeit,* and *weird.* These words will be taught in Level 5.

Point to the wr tile.   `wr`

"This tile says **/r/, two-letter /r/ used only at the beginning of a word**. Repeat after me: /r/, two-letter /r/ used only at the beginning of a word." *Student repeats.*

Point to the kn tile.   `kn`

"This tile says **/n/, two-letter /n/ used only at the beginning of a word**. Repeat after me: /n/, two-letter /n/ used only at the beginning of a word." *Student repeats.*

> Store the new tiles under the following labels:
>
> | Vowel Teams | Consonant Teams |
> |---|---|
> | `ew` `ei` | `tch` `dge` |

Step 5: Prefixes   35

New Teaching
(continued)

Take out Phonogram Cards 56, 57, 58, and 59 and practice them with your student.

Practice Sound Cards 64, 65, 66, and 67 with your student. Dictate the sound and have your student write the phonogram.

File the cards behind the appropriate Review dividers in the Spelling Review Box.

Teach Key Card 22: Prefixes

> A **prefix** is a word part placed in front of a base word to make a new word.

Build the word *happy*.

"I'm going to change the meaning of this word by adding a **prefix** in front of it." Place prefix *un* in front of *happy*.

"The prefix *un* means *not* or *the opposite of*. It changes the meaning of *happy* to *not happy*."

"Today you are going to learn more prefixes. The prefix *re* is one example. We can add *re* to the word *charge*."

"*Re* means *again*, so this word means *charge again*."

"*Re* is the **prefix**, and *charge* is the **base word**."

Read Key Card 22 with your student and then file it behind the Review divider.

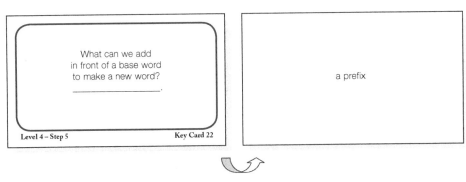

Step 5: Prefixes

New Teaching
(continued)

Place the prefix tiles on the table. "Let's use these prefixes to spell words."

"I am going to dictate some words. First choose the correct prefix tile, then spell the base word with tiles."

nonstop	**overfill**	**presoak**	**unthankful**
reprint	**semicircle**	**misstep**	

"Notice that we just add the prefix to the word—we don't change the prefix or the base word. In the word *misstep*, there are two s's in a row, and that is correct. We keep the s from the prefix *mis*, and we keep the s from the word *step*."

> **New!** Using prefix tiles instead of regular tiles in the prefix activities will help your student easily recognize the role of prefixes in spelling.

Teach Syllable Division Rule #5

Build the word *preplan* with tiles. "When a word has a prefix, the prefix forms a separate syllable. We can divide the word into syllables by dividing it after the prefix."

Take out the Syllable Division Rules Chart. "This is the fifth syllable division rule." Read Rule #5 with your student.

Have your student practice this rule by dividing the following words:

unpack **resell** **misjudge**

Step 5: Prefixes

Reinforcement

There are no new Word Cards for Step 5.

More Words

The following words reinforce the concepts taught in Step 5. To give your student more practice with recognizing and adding prefixes, first have him spell the words using the prefix and letter tiles.

semicircle	**preplan**	**rethink**	**unhappy**
nonmelting	**mistrust**	**revote**	**unharmful**
unpack	**semiweekly**	**resold**	**oversee**
preorder	**misprint**	**rename**	**preplanning**
uneventful	**unripe**	**unending**	

overdo (Don't overdo it!)   **overdue** (My library book is overdue.)

Dictate Sentences

Dictate several sentences each day.

The students sat in a semicircle.
The game was uneventful.
I don't like unripe bananas!
They resold the house.
We should rethink that plan!
Did you rename your goat?
A little preplanning will help us.
I think this word is a misprint.
Did you unpack your shirts?
We are overdue for a snack!
Did you preorder the pizza?
Are you unhappy when it rains?

Writing Station

Dictate each word and have your student write it on paper. Then have your student write original sentences using the new words.

judging	**contests**
retry	**pulling**
unlucky	

Step 5: Prefixes

Step 6 - The Four Sounds of Y

In this lesson, your student will categorize the four sounds of the letter y.

You will need: Y Word Sheet, Spelling Strategies Chart, Word Cards 21-30

Cut apart the words on the Y Word Sheet before beginning this lesson.

Review

New Teaching **Introduce Y Sorting Activity**

Take out the words from the Y Word Sheet, which you cut apart earlier.

Set out the following words:

| yellow | myth | shy | candy |

"You know that y has four sounds. Tell me the four sounds."
/y/–/ĭ/–/ī/–/ē/.

"In the word *yellow*, which sound does y make?" /y/.

"In the word *myth*, which sound does it make?" /ĭ/.

"Is *myth* an open or closed syllable?" *Closed.*

"Right. When y is in a closed syllable, it says its short sound."

"In the word *shy*, which sound does y make?" /ī/.

"What about in the word *candy*?" /ē/.

Step 6: The Four Sounds of Y

New Teaching
(continued)

> In words of Greek origin, the letter y is sometimes used in the middle of the word and sounds like the letter i would in the same location. For example, in a closed syllable the y has a short i sound, as in *gymnasium, myth, rhythm, hymn,* and *physical*. In a VCE syllable, it has a long i sound, as in *style, enzyme,* and *analyze*.

"In the words *shy* and *candy*, is y in an open or closed syllable?" *Open*.

"Right. If y is in an open syllable, it can say /ī/ or /ē/. What is the most common sound of y?" */ē/*.

"Good."

Take out the word *type*. | type |

"Sometimes y can be found in a vowel-consonant-e syllable. Silent E makes the y say /ī/. What is this word?" *Type*.

"Good. You know that y can also be part of a vowel team. Pull down the three tiles that show y in a vowel team." *Student pulls down the ay, ey, and oy letter tiles.*

"Right. Y can be in the ay vowel team, as in *stay*." | ay |

"It can be in the ey vowel team, as in *they*." | ey |

"And it can be in the oy vowel team, as in *boy*." | oy |

Lay out the five headings from the Y Word Sheet.

| Y in *yard* | | Y in *gym* | | Y in *cry* |

| Y in *puppy* | | Vowel Team |

"Here are the four different sounds of y, plus the vowel teams." Read the headings with your student.

"We will sort some words under the correct headings." Use the words from the Y Word Sheet.

Walk the student through the first several words.
  1. Read the word.
  2. Decide which sound y makes in the word.
  3. Put the word under the correct heading.

> The y in the word *puppy* is most commonly pronounced like long e, but in some areas it is pronounced like short i. You may need to adjust the wording in this lesson according to how you pronounce the last sound in *puppy*.

> **Tip!** You can adapt this activity for younger children by working with just three headings at a time.

New Teaching (continued)

Practice Spelling Strategies #1 and #2

Take out Word Cards 21-29 and the Spelling Strategies Chart. With your student, discuss spelling strategies that will help him spell the words. Some words may require the Pronounce for Spelling strategy, and others may require the Analyze the Word strategy.

Teach a Rule Breaker

Build the word *pretty*.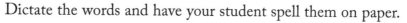

"In the word *pretty*, which letters don't say the sounds we expect them to say?" Lead your student to see that the e sounds like /ĭ/ and the t's sound like /d/.

Take out Word Card 30. "The word *pretty* is a Rule Breaker. Circle the e and the t's in this word, because they don't make the sounds we expect them to make." *Student fills in the circles with yellow pencil.*

"Spell the word *pretty* on paper." *Student spells the word.*

Word Cards 21-30: Spell on Paper

Dictate the words and have your student spell them on paper.

21. reply
22. destroy
23. yesterday
24. easy
25. gym   I lift weights at the gym.
26. family
27. story
28. history
29. type
30. pretty

File the Word Cards behind the Review divider.

Step 6: The Four Sounds of Y

Reinforcement

More Words

The following words reinforce the concepts taught in Step 6. Have your student spell them for additional practice.

    every   **everything**   **myth**   **study**

Homophone Pairs

Have your student add the following homophone pair to the Homophones List.

    gym / Jim

Read the following sentences and have your student point to the correct word on the Homophones List.

- **Let's go with Jim and Ben.**
- **The gym at school is really big.**
- **Jim is playing a game in the gym.**

Dictate Sentences

Dictate several sentences each day.

- **Did you reply to the teacher?**
- **What a pretty skirt!**
- **We must study everything tonight.**
- **The test should be easy.**
- **Shall we go to the gym?**
- **I am reading my family history.**
- **Did the dog destroy your book?**
- **Tom told us a story yesterday.**
- **I like every type of cake.**
- **Did you clean everything in the kitchen?**
- **I want to read that myth.**
- **Every girl at school is pretty!**

Reinforcement
(continued)

Writing Station

Dictate each word and have your student write it on paper. Then have your student write original sentences using the new words.

studying **reread** (present tense)

stories **overdue** (overdue books)

myths

Step 6: The Four Sounds of Y

Step 7 - The /er/ of Works

This lesson will teach words with the sound of /er/ as in works.

You will need: purple <u>or</u> letter tile, Phonogram Card 60, Sound Card 68, Word Bank for WOR, Word Cards 31-40

Review

New Teaching **Teach Another Way to Spell /er/**

"Pull down the tiles that make the sound of /er/." *Student pulls down* <u>er</u>, <u>ur</u>, *and* <u>ir</u>.

"Today we have another tile that makes the sound of /er/." Take out the purple <u>or</u> letter tile.

> Just like we need two <u>y</u> tiles, we need two <u>or</u> tiles. <u>Y</u> and <u>or</u> are the only two tiles that are represented in two colors.

"This tile says **/er/, as in *works*.** Repeat after me: /er/, as in *works*." *Student repeats.*

Build the word *works*. | w | or | k | s |

Now build the word *fork* with the yellow <u>or</u> tile.

"This word also uses an <u>or</u> tile. This is the tile you are used to using. What does <u>or</u> say in this word?" */or/.*

"The <u>or</u> usually says /or/, except when it comes after a <u>w</u>. After a <u>w</u>, it usually says /er/."

Move the yellow <u>or</u> tile back under the Other Tiles label.

Move all of the purple tiles back under the Sound of /er/ label. "We keep the purple <u>or</u> tile with the other tiles that spell the sound of /er/."

Step 7: The /er/ of *Works*

New Teaching
(continued)

> Now that your student has learned the second sound of <u>or</u>, Phonogram Card 37 and Sound Card 37 from Level 2 should be removed from the Spelling Review Box. Replace those cards with Phonogram Card 60 and Sound Card 68.

Teach Phonogram Card 60 and Sound Card 68

Take out Phonogram Card 60 and practice it with your student.

"Now we have two sounds for this card. Repeat after me: /or/–/er/ as in *works*." *Student repeats.*

Practice Sound Card 68 with your student. Dictate the sound and have your student write the phonogram.

File the cards behind the appropriate Review dividers in the Spelling Review Box.

Teach Words with the WOR Pattern

"Repeat these words after me, and listen for the /er/ sound: *word, work, worst, world.*" *Student listens and repeats the words.*

"I will dictate some words for you to spell. In each one, the /er/ sound comes after a <u>w</u>, so you will use the purple <u>or</u> tile."

Dictate the following words and have your student spell them with tiles:

worm　　　**work**　　　**worth**

Build the word *worry*.　| w | or | r | y |

"In the word *worry*, we double the <u>r</u>."

> If your student asks why the <u>r</u> is doubled, explain that we do so to protect the <u>o</u> and keep it short. If there were just one <u>r</u>, the <u>y</u> would "pull" it away and leave the <u>o</u> open.

Introduce the Word Bank for WOR

Have your student read through the **Word Bank for WOR** to improve visual memory. We want students to become very familiar with the words in this Word Bank before another spelling for /er/ is introduced.

New Teaching
(continued)

Teach Three Rule Breakers

Build the word *busy*. [b][u][s][y]

"The word *busy* is a Rule Breaker. Which letter doesn't say the sound we expect it to say?" *The u because it says /ĭ/.*

Take out Word Card 40. "What do we do with Rule Breakers?" *Student circles the u and colors in the circle with yellow pencil.*

"Write the word *busy*." *Student writes the word.*

Build the word *half*. [h][a][l][f]

"This is the word *half*. Look at the word and listen carefully as I say it: *half*. What do you notice about the pronunciation of this word?" *You don't pronounce the l.*

"Right. The l is silent in this word."

Build the word *talk*. [t][a][l][k]

"Here is another word with a silent l. What is this word?" *Talk.*

"*Half* and *talk* are Rule Breakers because the l doesn't say the sound we expect it to say."

Take out Word Cards 38 and 39. "Circle the l in these words." *Student circles the letters and colors in the circles with yellow pencil.*

"Write the words *half* and *talk*." *Student writes the words.*

Step 7: The /er/ of *Works*

New Teaching
(continued)

Word Cards 31-40: Spell on Paper

Dictate the words and have your student spell them on paper.

31.	word	Can you spell this word?
32.	work	
33.	world	The world is round.
34.	worth	
35.	worm	
36.	worst	
37.	worry	
38.	half	
39.	talk	
40.	busy	

Even though *word* and *world* have homophones, the pairs will not be added to the Homophones List because your student has not yet learned how to spell *whirred* and *whirled*.

File the Word Cards behind the Review divider.

Reinforcement

More Words

The following words reinforce the concepts taught in Step 7. Have your student spell them for additional practice.

words   **walk**

48   Step 7: The /er/ of *Works*

Reinforcement
(continued)

Dictate Sentences

Dictate several sentences each day.

> That worm is only one inch long.
> I work hard all day.
> You worry too much!
> Half of the babies are crying!
> The world is mostly made of water.
> This is the worst apple in the bunch!
> I need to talk to my uncle.
> Walk to the mall with me.
> How much is his boat worth?
> Who is studying on the porch?
> Which words did you spell right?
> Did you reread those myths?

Writing Station

Dictate each word and have your student write it on paper. Then have your student write original sentences using the new words.

replies
typing
mail (mail a letter)
aunt (Aunt Sue)
dear (dear to me)

Step 7: The /er/ of *Works*

Step 8 - Months of the Year

In this lesson, your student will learn how to spell the months of the year and write common abbreviations.

You will need: calendar (optional), Word Cards 41-50

Review

Word Bank for WOR

New Teaching

Teach the Months of the Year

"Tell me the months of the year." *Student responds.*

If your student doesn't know the months of the year in order, take out a calendar and go through them together.

Write the word *July* on paper.

"Remember that all months start with a capital letter. Keep that in mind as we build these words with tiles. When you write them on paper, use a capital letter."

Point to the letter y. "What sound does the letter y have in this word?" /ī/.

Build the word *January*.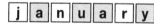

"Read this word." *January.*

Build the word *February*. [f][e][b][r][u][a][r][y]

As *February* is commonly mispronounced, have your student read the word slowly and carefully, being sure to "pronounce for spelling": /feb/–/roo/–/ār/–/ē/.

> Note that we are not using the <u>ar</u> tile to build *January* and *February* because the final <u>a</u> in those words says long <u>a</u>.

Tip! By the end of this Step your student will know how to spell the names of all twelve months. Since *March, April, May, June,* and *August* were taught in previous levels, you may wish to review those words by having the student spell all twelve months in order.

New Teaching
(continued)

Build the word *December*.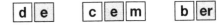

"Read this word." *December.*

"Divide this word into syllables." *Student divides the word.*

| d | e | | c | e | m | | b | er |

"In the second syllable, what letter says /s/?" *The c.*

"How do we spell the /er/ sound?" *Er.*

"When you hear the sound of /er/ in one of the twelve months, spell it with the er tile."

Teach *Mr.* and *Mrs.*

"An **abbreviation** is a shortened form of a word. Repeat this word: *abbreviation*." *Student repeats the word.*

Write *Mister* and *Mr.* on a piece of paper.

"*Mr.* is a shortened way of writing the word *Mister*. Notice that in this abbreviation, we capitalize the m and add a period at the end. Write the abbreviation *Mr.*, as in *Mr. Brown*." *Student writes the word.*

Write *Missus* and *Mrs.* on a piece of paper.

"*Mrs.* is a shortened way of writing the word *Missus*. What two things do we have to do when we make this abbreviation?" *Give it a capital m and put a period at the end.*

"Good. Write the abbreviation *Mrs.*, as in *Mrs. Brown*." *Student writes the word.*

> Students may ask where the r in *Mrs.* comes from if the abbreviation stands for *Missus*. The r is left over from the days when *Mrs.* was an abbreviation for *Mistress*, which used to be the title of respect for women. Though we now say *Missus* instead of *Mistress*, the r in *Mrs.* has remained.

New Teaching
(continued)

Teach a Rule Breaker

Build the word *eye*.

"This is the word *eye*. What sound does the <u>e-y</u> make in this word?" *Long i.*

Take out Word Card 50. "Right. The word *eye* is a Rule Breaker because the <u>e-y</u> says /ī/ instead of /ā/ like we expect it to. What do we do with Rule Breakers?" *Student circles the <u>e-y</u> and colors in the circle with yellow pencil.*

"Write the word *eye*." *Student writes the word.*

Word Cards 41-50: Spell on Paper

Dictate the words and have your student spell them on paper.

41. January
42. February
43. July
44. September
45. October
46. November
47. December
48. Mr.
49. Mrs.   Mrs. Brown is my teacher.
50. eye   Don't shine the light in my eye.

File the Word Cards behind the Review divider.

Step 8: Months of the Year

Reinforcement

More Words

If you are working with an older student, this is a good time to teach the abbreviations for the months of the year.

Jan.	Feb.	Mar.	Apr.	Aug.
Sept.	Oct.	Nov.	Dec.	

Note that *May*, *June*, and *July* are already short enough and therefore do not have abbreviations!

Homophone Pairs

Have your student add the following homophone pairs to the Homophones List.

          eye / I   **Mrs. / misses**

Read the following sentences and have your student point to the correct word on the Homophones List.

My dog <u>misses</u> me when I'm gone.
Your right <u>eye</u> is very red!
<u>I</u> will wash the dishes tonight.
<u>Mrs.</u> Brown gave us too much homework!

Reinforcement
(continued)

Dictate Sentences

Dictate several sentences each day.

February is the coldest time of the year.
Mrs. Brown will come in July.
I am happy when school starts in September!
I have one blue eye and one green eye.
Who will you vote for in November?
Did you get any replies in the mail?
The lakes are icy in December.
Did it snow last October?
Don't walk on the edge of the road.
She is very busy typing the report.
Is Mr. Brown chopping down the tree today?
What will he do with the branches?

Writing Station

Dictate each word and have your student write it on paper. Then have your student write original sentences using the new words.

roads   **bridges**
working   **walking**
edges

Are any words giving your student trouble? If so, review the article "Learn How to Handle Troublemakers" on page 8. **Tip!**

After a word has been misspelled and subsequently corrected, dictate the word later in the spelling lesson. Come back to it several times that day, and write a note to yourself to review that word again the next day.

Customizing your student's instruction in this way will help his spelling ability grow more quickly.

Step 8: Months of the Year

Step 9 - The Sound of /ōō/ Spelled EW

In this lesson, your student will learn to spell words containing the sound of /ōō/ spelled ew.

You will need: Word Bank for EW, Word Cards 51-60

Review

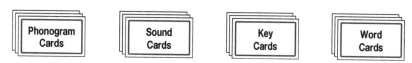

Word Bank for WOR

Are you remembering to shuffle the Word Cards before dictating them? Dictate review words with a variety of patterns.

New Teaching

Depending upon the needs of your student, you can have him spell on paper or with the letter tiles.

Teach the Sound of /ōō/ Spelled EW

"Repeat these words after me and listen for the /ōō/ sound: *chew, threw, drew, grew.*" *Student listens and repeats the words.*

"I will dictate some words for you to spell. In each one, the /ōō/ sound is spelled *ew*."

Dictate the following words:

flew **new** **screw** **dew**

Introduce the Word Bank for EW

Have your student read through the **Word Bank for EW** to improve visual memory. There are several ways to spell the sound of /ōō/ and we want students to become very familiar with the words in this Word Bank. This will enable the student to choose the correct spelling of /ōō/ when he needs to spell one of these words.

Step 9: The Sound of /ōō/ Spelled EW

New Teaching
(continued)

Why are Word Banks so important? Take the current sound, /ōō/, for example. So far your student has learned six ways to spell the sound of /ōō/:

1. u as in *unit*
2. u-e as in *June*
3. o as in *do*
4. oo as in *food*
5. ou as in *you*
6. ew as in *flew*

Later in the program, students will learn three more ways to spell the sound of /ōō/:

7. u-e as in *due*
8. ough as in *through*
9. ui as in *fruit*

That's a lot of information for the student to hold onto! With so many options for spelling this sound and many others, you can see how important it is to build your student's visual memory of each spelling of a sound.

Teach *Their*

Build the word *their*.

"This word says *their*, as in *That is their house*. What sound does <u>ei</u> have in the word *their*?" /ā/.

"*Their* means *belonging to them*."

Dictate the following phrases to help your student understand the proper usage of the word *their* and to give him practice writing it.

their green car

in their yard

their puppy

at their party

Mixed practice with the words *their* and *there* will be provided in the Homophone Pairs and Dictate Sentences sections of the lesson.

Step 9: The Sound of /ōō/ Spelled EW

New Teaching (continued)

Word Cards 51-60: Spell on Paper

Dictate the words and have your student spell them on paper.

51. few
52. new — I bought a new coat.
53. chew
54. grew
55. flew — The bird flew away.
56. threw — Bob threw the ball.
57. newspaper
58. blew — The baby blew bubbles.
59. drew
60. their — Their dog has fleas.

File the Word Cards behind the Review divider.

Reinforcement

More Words

The following words reinforce the concepts taught in Step 9. Have your student spell them for additional practice.

news   **screw**
stew   **dew** (There's dew on the grass.)

Step 9: The Sound of /ōō/ Spelled EW

Reinforcement
(continued)

Homophone Pairs

Have your student add the following homophone pairs to the Homophones List.

    their / there   blew / blue   dew / do / due

Read the following sentences and have your student point to the correct word on the Homophones List.

Would you stand over there, please?
Pam blew up the balloon.
Is that their car?
Do you have a pencil?
She lives in a blue house.
The sun shines on the morning dew.
Their cat is brown and white.
My library book is due tomorrow.

Dictate Sentences

Dictate several sentences each day.

Could you catch the balls she threw?
There is a party at their house tonight.
He ate a spoonful of stew.
Sue drew a sketch for Tom.
I need a new screw for my bike.
A few planes flew in the sky.
I love the morning dew!
Did the goat chew up their yellow flowers?
My sister grew two inches this year.
The baby blew big bubbles.
I saw the story in the newspaper.
Did you hear the news?

Reinforcement
(continued)

Writing Station

Dictate each word and have your student write it on paper. Then have your student write original sentences using the new words.

newest **four** (number four)
prizes **won** (won the race)
races

Step 9: The Sound of /ōō/ Spelled EW

Step 10 - Short E Spelled EA

In this lesson, your student will learn to spell words containing the sound of /ĕ/ spelled ea.

You will need: Word Bank for EA (/ĕ/), Word Cards 61-70

Review

Word Bank for EW

New Teaching   **Teach Another Way to Spell /ĕ/**

Build the word *ever*.

Point to the first <u>e</u>. "The most common way to spell the sound of /ĕ/ is with the letter <u>e</u>, as in the word *ever*."

"You have also learned another phonogram that makes the sound of /ĕ/. Pull down that tile." *Student pulls down the <u>ea</u> tile.*

"Today we will work on spelling words with the sound of /ĕ/ spelled <u>ea</u>."

Build the word *deaf*.   d ea f

Point to the <u>ea</u> tile. "What sound does this tile have in this word?" /ĕ/.

"Using this tile, spell the word *read*, as in *I read the book yesterday*." *Student spells the word with tiles.*

"I will dictate some words for you to spell. The /ĕ/ sound in these words is spelled with the <u>ea</u> tile."

Dictate the following words:

bread   **health**   **ready**   **instead**

Step 10: Short E Spelled EA

New Teaching
(continued)

Introduce the Word Bank for EA (/ĕ/)

Have your student read through the **Word Bank for EA (/ĕ/)** to improve visual memory. There are several ways to spell the sound of /ĕ/ and we want students to become very familiar with the words in this Word Bank. This will enable the student to choose the correct spelling of short e when he needs to spell one of these words.

Spotlight on Silent E

Spell the word *tie* with tiles.

"The word *tie* ends in Silent E. What is the job of Silent E in this word?" *It keeps i from being the last letter, because English words don't end in i.*

Word Cards 61-70: Spell on Paper

Dictate the words and have your student spell them on paper.

61. **dead**
62. **ready**
63. **weather**   What beautiful weather!
64. **instead**
65. **health**
66. **bread**   Sue ate some bread and jam.
67. **deaf**
68. **die**   Those flowers will die without water.
69. **pie**
70. **tie**

File the Word Cards behind the Review divider.

Step 10: Short E Spelled EA

Reinforcement

More Words

The following words reinforce the concepts taught in Step 10. Have your student spell them for additional practice.

spread **lead** (Lead is a type of metal.)
lie **read** (Bob read the newspaper.)
head

Homophone Pairs

Have your student add the following homophone pairs to the Homophones List.

lead / led   **read / red**

Read the following sentences and have your student point to the correct word on the Homophones List.

There's no lead in my pencil.
I have a red backpack.
Jim led his team to victory.
My teacher read the story out loud.
The weights at the gym are made of lead.

Dictate Sentences

Dictate several sentences each day.

I read that the weather would be stormy.
Is your aunt in good health?
There are twelve dead mice in the barn!
Please spread more jam on my bread.
Let's eat pie instead of bread.
Dad has a new blue tie on today.
My deaf cat is very cute and playful!
Did they tell a lie to Mike?
I'm ready to go sledding!
Did the hedges die from the cold?
Is there lead in your pencil?
My head is full of stories!

Reinforcement
(continued)

Writing Station

Dictate each word and have your student write it on paper. Then have your student write original sentences using the new words.

pies   **premade**
healthy   **would** (would win)
easily

 How is the daily review going? Are the decks behind the Mastered dividers getting bigger?

Mastered cards will be reviewed in Step 13 to keep them fresh in your student's mind.

Step 11 - Ways to Spell /ĕ/

In this lesson, your student will analyze two ways to spell the sound of /ĕ/.

You will need: Spelling Strategies Chart, Sound Card 69

Review

Word Bank for EA (/ĕ/)
Word Bank for EW

New Teaching

Introduce the Word Sort for /ĕ/

Write these two headings across the top of lined paper. Draw vertical lines to form two columns:

e	ea

Point to the column headings. "Here are two ways to spell the sound of /ĕ/."

Give your student a new sheet of lined paper. "I will dictate a word and you will write it down on your paper. When you are satisfied that you have spelled the word correctly, copy the word to the correct column on this chart."

Dictate the following words:

yellow	instead	penny	bedding
weather	deaf	bread	head
helpful	forgiveness	melting	death
dentist	strongest	pencil	ready

New Teaching
(continued)

Discuss Spelling Strategy #3

"What you just did is called Scratch Paper Spelling. Sometimes, if you are unsure of how a word should be spelled, it helps to try it out on scratch paper. You can try spelling it several different ways until it 'looks right.'"

Take out the Spelling Strategies Chart and review Strategy #3 with your student.

Teach Sound Card 69

"Today we have a new Sound Card."

Read Sound Card 69:

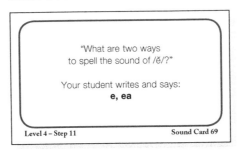

Practice this Sound Card with your student and then store it behind the Review divider.

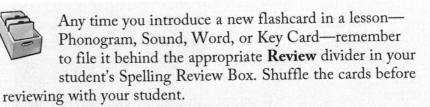

Any time you introduce a new flashcard in a lesson—Phonogram, Sound, Word, or Key Card—remember to file it behind the appropriate **Review** divider in your student's Spelling Review Box. Shuffle the cards before reviewing with your student.

If your student doesn't hesitate on a flashcard during the daily review, that card is ready to be filed behind the appropriate **Mastered** divider.

Reinforcement

There are no new Word Cards for Step 11.

Dictate Sentences

Dictate several sentences each day.

How many prizes did you win?
The edges of my coat are dirty.
We'll never go to the car races.
There are seven bridges in my town.
I found the clue easily.
Those broken printers are worthless.
I enjoy walking the dog.
She baked fifty sticky plum pies.
He is a very unlucky boy!
The snail passed me silently.
Apples are sweet and healthy.
Why are you pulling a pig on a rope?

Writing Station

Dictate each word and have your student write it on paper. Then have your student write original sentences using the new words.

preheat   **overfilling**
thawing   **two** (two cookies)
slowly

Step 11: Ways to Spell /ĕ/

Step 12 - The Sound of /r/ Spelled WR

In this lesson, your student will learn to spell words containing the sound of /r/ spelled wr.

You will need: Word Cards 71-80

Review

Word Bank for EA (/ĕ/)
Word Bank for WOR

New Teaching   **Teach the Sound of /r/ Spelled WR**

"Pull down /r/, two-letter /r/ used only at the beginning of a word." *Student pulls down the wr tile.*

Build the word *write*. | wr | i | t | e |

"In the word *write*, as in *write a letter*, the /r/ sound is spelled *wr*."

"Repeat these words after me, and listen for the /r/ sound: *wrestle, wrist, wrote, wrap*." *Student listens and repeats the words.*

"I will dictate some words for you to spell. In each one, the /r/ sound at the beginning of the word is spelled *wr*."

Dictate the following words:

wrist   **wrap**   **wrote**   **wrong**

> **Tip!** Words beginning with *wr* often have to do with twisting, as in *wrist, wrestle, wreath, wrench, wringer, wrap,* and *wrapper*.
>
> Even the word *wrong*, which has the same roots as the other words and means something that isn't quite "straight," easily fits into this category.
>
> To enhance their memory of *wr* words, some students find it useful (and fun!) to act out a twisting motion as they say each of the *wr* words.

New Teaching
(continued)

Teach Some Compound Words

"Now let's learn some new compound words. These compound words contain two smaller words that you already know how to spell."

Dictate the following words:

afternoon	**something**	**understand**
anything	**sometimes**	

Word Cards 71-80: Spell on Paper

Dictate the words and have your student spell them on paper.

71. **write** — Write me a letter.
72. **wrote** — Ted wrote an essay.
73. **wrap** — Please wrap the food in foil.
74. **wrist**
75. **wrong**
76. **afternoon**
77. **something**
78. **understand**
79. **anything**
80. **sometimes**

File the Word Cards behind the Review divider.

Reinforcement

More Words

The following words reinforce the concepts taught in Step 12. Have your student spell them for additional practice.

anyway   **wrench**

Reinforcement
(continued)

Homophone Pairs

Have your student add the following homophone pair to the Homophones List.

write / right

Read the following sentences and have your student point to the correct word on the Homophones List.

   Did you <u>write</u> a letter to Aunt Beth?
   My <u>right</u> hand is smaller than my left hand.
   Turn <u>right</u> at the candy store.
   I like to <u>write</u> poetry.

Dictate Sentences

Dictate several sentences each day.

   Write a cheerful song for me.
   Did you wrap the birthday gifts in purple paper?
   Can you pay for anything with pennies?
   Use a wrench to fix the clock.
   I got three words wrong in the spelling contest.
   I didn't want to win a prize anyway!
   I broke my wrist when I was thirteen.
   Sometimes I wish I could be a catfish.
   I would swim in clear water all afternoon!
   Jim cannot understand me when I speak.
   Something made a noise behind me.
   Mrs. Brown wrote a long book.

Writing Station

Dictate each word and have your student write it on paper. Then have your student write original sentences using the new words.

   hilltops   **deer** (family of deer)
   chewing   **there** (over there)
   sketched

Step 12: The Sound of /r/ Spelled WR

Step 13 - The Sound of /n/ Spelled KN

In this lesson, your student will learn words that contain the sound of /n/ spelled kn.

You will need: Word Cards 81-90

Review

Word Bank for EW

 Quickly review the cards behind the Mastered dividers.

New Teaching **Teach the Sound of /n/ Spelled KN**

"Pull down /n/, two-letter /n/ used only at the beginning of a word." *Student pulls down the kn tile.*

Build the word *know*.

"In the word *know*, as in *I don't know*, the /n/ sound is spelled <u>kn</u>."

"Repeat these words after me, and listen for the /n/ sound: *knee, knot, know, knife*." *Student listens and repeats the words.*

"I will dictate some words for you to spell. In each one, the /n/ sound at the beginning of the word is spelled <u>kn</u>."

Dictate the following words:

    knock   **knight**   **knit**   **kneel**

Step 13: The Sound of /n/ Spelled KN

New Teaching
(continued)

Teach Two Rule Breakers

Build the word *sure*. [s][u][r][e]

"This word is *sure*. What sound does the s make in this word?" */sh/.*

Take out Word Card 89. "The word *sure* is a Rule Breaker because the s says /sh/ instead of /s/. Circle the s in this word." *Student fills in the circle with yellow pencil.*

"Spell the word *sure* on paper." *Student writes the word.*

Build the word *says*. [s][ay][s]

"This word is *says*, as in *He always says no*. What is the base word of *says*?" *Say.*

"Good. But what sound does the ay make in the word *says*?" */ĕ/.*

Take out Word Card 90. "The word *says* is a Rule Breaker because the ay doesn't say what we expect it to. What do we do with Rule Breakers?" *The student circles the ay and colors the circle yellow.*

"Spell the word *says* on paper." *Student writes the word.*

Have your student practice these two words until they become easy.

Word Cards 81-90: Spell on Paper

Dictate the words and have your student spell them on paper.

81.	know	Do you know how to ski?
82.	knew	I knew all the answers!
83.	knee	
84.	knife	
85.	knit	Sue can knit sweaters very well.
86.	knock	
87.	knot	I tied my shoelaces in a knot.
88.	knight	The knight rode on a white horse.
89.	sure	
90.	says	

File the Word Cards behind the Review divider.

Reinforcement

More Words

The following words reinforce the concepts taught in Step 13. Have your student spell them for additional practice.

    kneel   **known**

Homophone Pairs

Have your student add the following homophone pairs to the Homophones List.

    know / no   **knot / not**   **knight / night**   **knew / new**

Read the following sentences and have your student point to the correct word on the Homophones List.

    Ted did <u>not</u> do his homework.
    The moon was full last <u>night</u>.
    The <u>knight</u> wore heavy armor.
    Is that a <u>new</u> sweater?
    Do you <u>know</u> my cousin Bob?
    The sailor tied the rope in a <u>knot</u>.
    I <u>knew</u> you'd like that pony!
    There are <u>no</u> more cookies in the jar.

Dictate Sentences

Dictate several sentences each day.

    Rick stuck the knife in the wood.
    He's the kindest man I've ever known.
    I knew you could do it!
    The brave knight helped the king.
    Knock three times on the window.
    Do you know how to knit?
    The frozen food is thawing on the table.
    I hurt my knee when I fell off the bed.
    Tie a knot in the fishing wire.
    Are you sure you want to kneel in the mud?
    Preheat the oven to cook the beef.
    Kim didn't know the ring belonged to Beth.

Step 13: The Sound of /n/ Spelled KN

Reinforcement
(continued)

Writing Station

Dictate each word and have your student write it on paper. Then have your student write original sentences using the new words.

sunniest **bee** (honey bee)
worker **their** (their house)
busier

Step 14 - More ER Words

In this lesson, your student will learn more words containing er.

You will need: Word Bank for ER, Word Cards 91-100

Review

Phonogram Cards Sound Cards Key Cards Word Cards

Word Bank for EA (/ĕ/)

New Teaching

Teach a Rule Breaker

Build the word *friend*.

"In the word *friend*, which letter doesn't say what we expect it to?" *The i.*

"Right. The i is not pronounced in this word."

Take out Word Card 100. "The word *friend* is a Rule Breaker. Circle the i in this word, because it doesn't make the sound we expect it to make." *Student fills in the circle with yellow pencil.*

"Spell the word *friend* on paper." *Student spells the word.*

Introduce the Word Bank for ER

Pull down the er letter tile.

"As you know, er is the most common way to spell the sound of /er/."

Take out the Word Bank for ER. "Read the words in this Word Bank and listen for the /er/ sound."

"Er can be part of the base word, like in the word *serve*, or it can be a suffix."

Step 14: More ER Words

New Teaching
(continued)

Jobs can also end in suffix *or* (as in *doctor, illustrator, navigator*), but suffix *er* is more common.

Point to the words *farmer* and *jogger* on the Word Bank. "A farmer is someone who farms. A *jogger* is someone who jogs. See if you can find other words where suffix *er* is added to mean someone who." *Student points to words such as* banker, walker, *and* driver.

"Name something in this room that is **bigger** than a pencil." *Student names an item.*

"Who do you think runs **faster**, you or me?" *Student responds.*

"We were just comparing two things. Words like *bigger, faster,* and *hotter* are all used in comparisons. Comparisons end in suffix *er*. See if you can find other comparisons ending in suffix *er* on this list." *Student points to some comparison words.*

Spotlight on Silent E

Point to the word *serve* on the Word Bank for ER. "The word *serve* ends in Silent E. What is the job of Silent E in this word?" *It keeps v from being the last letter because English words don't end in v (or, it keeps v from tipping over).*

New Teaching
(continued)

Word Cards 91-100: Spell on Paper

Dictate the words and have your student spell them on paper.

91. summer
92. father
93. serve
94. offer
95. prefer
96. refer
97. power
98. better
99. letter
100. friend

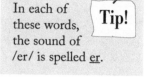

Tip! In each of these words, the sound of /er/ is spelled er.

File the Word Cards behind the Review divider.

Reinforcement

More Words

The following words reinforce the concepts taught in Step 14. Have your student spell them for additional practice.

however   matter

Reinforcement
(continued)

Dictate Sentences

Dictate several sentences each day.

> I would prefer to eat lunch later.
> The worker knew how to make maple candy.
> You can reply however you like.
> Today was the sunniest day of summer!
> Did your best friend write you a letter?
> What's the matter with Sue?
> The mean queen had too much power.
> Be sure to serve ice with those drinks.
> Ben is a better painter than Beth.
> Did you offer to read to the old lady?
> You should refer to a map if you are lost.
> My sister says she is busier than a bee.

Writing Station

Dictate each word and have your student write it on paper. Then have your student write original sentences using the new words.

hedges   **armful**
grassy   **flowers**
clipped

Your student is halfway there! Has he been filling out his Progress Chart?

Step 15 - The Sound of /ŭ/ Spelled O

In this lesson, your student will learn three new phonograms and how to spell words containing the sound of /ŭ/ spelled o.

You will need: letter tiles <u>eigh</u>, <u>ear</u>, and <u>ph</u>, Phonogram Cards 61-63, Sound Cards 70-72, Spelling Strategies Chart, Word Cards 101-110

Review

Word Bank for ER
Word Bank for WOR

New Teaching   **Teach New Phonograms EIGH, EAR, and PH**

"We have three new tiles today."

Point to the <u>eigh</u> tile.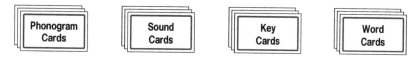

"This tile says **/ā/, four-letter /ā/**. Repeat after me: /ā/, four-letter /ā/." *Student repeats.*

Point to the <u>ear</u> tile.   `ear`

"This tile says **/er/, as in *early***. Repeat after me: /er/, as in *early*." *Student repeats.*

Point to the <u>ph</u> tile.   `ph`

"This tile says **/f/, two-letter /f/**. Repeat after me: /f/, two-letter /f/." *Student repeats.*

Store the new tiles under the following labels:

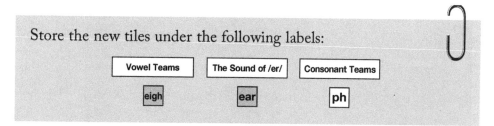

Step 15: The Sound of /ŭ/ Spelled O

New Teaching
(continued)

Take out Phonogram Cards 61, 62, and 63 and practice them with your student.

Practice Sound Cards 70, 71, and 72 with your student. Dictate the sound and have your student write the phonogram.

File the cards behind the appropriate Review dividers in the Spelling Review Box.

Teach the Sound of /ŭ/ Spelled O

Pull down the o tile. | o |

"Tell me the sounds of o." /ŏ/-/ō/-/o͞o/-/ŭ/.

Build the word *dozen*. | d | o | z | e | n |

"In this word, o says its fourth sound, /ŭ/. What is this word?" *Dozen*.

"Today you will learn words with the /ŭ/ sound. When you hear the sound of /ŭ/, spell it with the o tile."

Practice Spelling Strategies #1, #2, and #3

Take out Word Cards 101-110 and the Spelling Strategies Chart. With your student, discuss spelling strategies that will help him spell the words. Some words may require the Pronounce for Spelling strategy, and others may require the Analyze the Word or Scratch Paper Spelling strategies.

New Teaching
(continued)

Word Cards 101-110: Spell on Paper

Dictate the words and have your student spell them on paper.

101. person
102. mother
103. dozen
104. front
105. nothing
106. second
107. month
108. other
109. brother
110. done

File the Word Cards behind the Review divider.

Reinforcement

More Words

The following words reinforce the concepts taught in Step 15. Have your student spell them for additional practice.

cover　　　　**become**　　　　**income**

Step 15: The Sound of /ŭ/ Spelled O

Reinforcement
(continued)

Dictate Sentences

Dictate several sentences each day.

> Which person do you want on your team?
> A dozen moths flew into the light.
> I'll meet you in front of the log cabin.
> Are you done training the tiger?
> There is nothing left to say.
> The other sheep seem happier.
> Their father planted a tree on the grassy hill.
> I go to the dentist every month.
> Mrs. White has one brother and nine sisters.
> Give me a second to finish this letter.
> Frank will become a farmer.
> I gave my mother an armful of flowers.

Writing Station

Dictate each word and have your student write it on paper. Then have your student write original sentences using the new words.

cutest	eyes
sniffing	here (come here)
munching	

Step 16 - Practice Spelling Strategies

In this lesson, your student will apply spelling strategies to spell multisyllable words.

You will need: Spelling Strategies Chart, Word Cards 111-120

Review

Review Words with the Sound of /er/: From the Word Card Mastered deck, pull out all words that have the sound of /er/ and review them with your student. Shuffle the cards to mix up the different spellings of /er/.

New Teaching

Practice Spelling Strategies #1, #2, and #3

Build the word *important*, using the yellow <u>or</u> tile. Leave a blank red tile in place of the <u>a</u>.

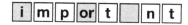

"I want to spell the word *important*."

> **Tip!** The muffled vowel sound is called a *schwa*, and it occurs in unaccented syllables. By saying the word aloud and stressing the syllable in which the schwa occurs, the vowel sound usually becomes clearer.

Point to the blank tile. "It is difficult to hear this vowel sound. It will be easier to hear it if I say this syllable louder, like this: *im–por–TANT*."

"What vowel sound did you hear?" /ă/.

"Good. We can hear the /ă/ sound, so we can put in the <u>a</u> tile."

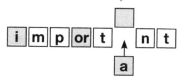

Take out the Spelling Strategies Chart and uncover the first three strategies. "Which one of these spelling strategies did we use to spell the word *important*?" *Pronounce for spelling.*

"Right. We exaggerated the pronunciation so that we could hear the /ă/ sound. We are going to use these strategies to spell the multisyllable words on today's word list."

New Teaching
(continued)

Take out Word Cards 111-119. Have your student read the words clearly and then practice spelling them on paper or with tiles. If your student has trouble spelling any of the words, have him use the spelling strategies that he has learned.

Teach a Rule Breaker

Build the word *women*.

Adjust the wording in this section to match the pronunciation in your region.

"In the word *women*, which letter doesn't say what we expect it to?" *The o.*

"Right. In this word, the o says /ĭ/."

Take out Word Card 120. "The word *women* is a Rule Breaker. Circle the o in this word, because it doesn't make the sound we expect it to make." *Student fills in the circle with yellow pencil.*

"Spell the word *women* on paper." *Student spells the word.*

Word Cards 111-120: Spell on Paper

Dictate the words and have your student spell them on paper.

111. interest
112. together
113. remember
114. surprise
115. complete
116. husband
117. important
118. different
119. woman
120. women

File the Word Cards behind the Review divider.

Reinforcement   **Dictate Sentences**

Dictate several sentences each day.

> Eating healthy food is so important!
> We could plan the trip together.
> Do you remember your childhood?
> Her new husband makes robots.
> You are overfilling the cup!
> She has no interest in sailing.
> The woman put on her red lipstick.
> What a surprise to see you here!
> Did you complete the task?
> Would you prefer something different?
> Cover your eyes and ears!
> Those two women sell candles.

Writing Station

Dictate each word and have your student write it on paper. Then have your student write original sentences using the new words.

rewrote	**reread** (past tense)
friendly	**for** (not for me)
letters	

Step 16: Practice Spelling Strategies

Step 17 - Words with EIGH and Numbers

In this lesson, your student will learn to spell words with eigh and numbers up to one hundred.

You will need: hyphen tile, Word Cards 121-130

Review

Word Bank for EW
Word Bank for EA (/ĕ/)

New Teaching

Teach Words with EIGH

Pull down the <u>eigh</u> tile.

"Tell me the sound of this tile." */ā/.*

"We use this tile to spell the word *eight*." Build the word with tiles.

"From the word *eight*, we can spell the words *eighteen* and *eighty*." Build the words.

"We can also add letters to <u>eigh</u> to make new words." Place the <u>eigh</u> tile in front of your student.

"Add a letter to this tile to make the word *weigh*, as in *How much do you weigh?*" Student adds a <u>w</u>.

"Good. Now add another letter to make the word *weight*, as in *He lifted the weight over his head.*" Student adds a <u>t</u>.

Step 17: Words with EIGH and Numbers

New Teaching
(continued)

"The word *neighbor* also uses the eigh tile. Which letters can you replace to spell the word *neighbor*? For spelling purposes, it helps to pronounce the word like *neigh–BOR*." *Student replaces the w and t with the appropriate letters.*

Teach Numbers Up to One Hundred

"You already know how to spell some numbers, like *six, fifty, twelve,* and *thirteen*. Today we will work on spelling more numbers."

Build the word *four*. | f | ou | r |

"You know that this is the word *four*. To make it into the word *fourteen*, we add the letters t-ee-n to the end of it." Build the word.

Dictate the following words and have your student spell them on paper. If necessary, tell your student that we do not add a second t in the word *eighteen*.

sixteen   **seventeen**   **eighteen**

Build the word *forty*. | f | or | t | y |

"What does this word say?" *Forty.*

"Right. We might expect the word *forty* to be spelled like the number *four*, but it isn't. We use the or tile to spell *forty*. Spell the word *forty* on paper." *Student writes the word.*

Build the word *twenty*. | t | w | e | n | t | y |

"This word says *twenty*. I will dictate some more words like this. When you hear the /tē/ sound at the end, be sure to spell it with t-y."

Dictate the following words and have your student spell them on paper.

twenty   **thirty**   **sixty**   **eighty**
seventy   **ninety**

New Teaching
(continued)

Using the hyphen tile, build the word *twenty-one*.

t w e n t y - o n e

"When we write numbers like *twenty-one*, we add a hyphen between the two words. I will dictate some more words like this. Be sure to add a hyphen between the words."

Dictate the following words and have your student spell them on paper.

seventy-five　　**ninety-three**　　**eighty-nine**
forty-four　　**fifty-six**

Build the word *hundred*.　h u n d r e d

"What is this word?" *Hundred*.

"Spell the word *hundred*." *Student spells the word on paper.*

Store the hyphen tile under the following label:

Other Tiles

-

Word Cards 121-130: Spell on Paper

Dictate the words and have your student spell them on paper.

121. eight　　She has eight marbles.
122. ninety
123. hundred
124. fourteen
125. eleven　　(Pronounce for spelling.)
126. eighteen
127. forty-four
128. seventy
129. twenty-eight
130. neighbor

File the Word Cards behind the Review divider.

Step 17: Words with EIGH and Numbers

Reinforcement

More Words

The following words reinforce the concepts taught in Step 17. Have your student spell them for additional practice.

sixteen	seventeen	weight	weigh
nineteen	twenty	eighty	forty

Homophone Pairs

Have your student add the following homophone pairs to the Homophones List.

eight / ate   weigh / way   weight / wait

Read the following sentences and have your student point to the correct word on the Homophones List.

Who <u>ate</u> all the apples?
I always have to <u>wait</u> for the bus.
Which <u>way</u> did he go?
Beth bought <u>eight</u> purple sweaters.
There's too much <u>weight</u> in this boat!
Did the vet <u>weigh</u> your cat?

Dictate Sentences

Dictate several sentences each day.

Ed will gladly eat twenty-eight oysters.
Don't forget to weigh the hens.
Eleven joggers tied for first place in the race.
Our noisy neighbor sings all afternoon.
Eight bands will play on the stage tonight.
They have forty-four pink marbles.
Is she fourteen or seventeen years old?
How much weight can you pick up?
A hundred ants crept up the wall.
You will finish school when you are eighteen.
My aunt keeps seventy or eighty acorns in a jar.
We reread those letters together.

New Teaching **Writing Station**

Dictate each word and have your student write it on paper. Then have your student write original sentences using the new words.

surprises   **ripping**
reaching   **wait** (wait for him)
wrapping

Step 17: Words with EIGH and Numbers

Step 18 - The Sounds of /ū/ and /ōō/ Spelled UE

In this lesson, your student will learn to spell more words containing the sounds of /ū/ and /ōō/ spelled ue and how to spell the days of the week.

You will need: Key Card 6 (first introduced in Level 2), Word Bank for UE, Word Cards 131-140, calendar (optional)

Review

Word Bank for WOR

New Teaching

Spotlight on Silent E

Take out Key Card 6 and review it with your student. "English words don't end in which letters?" *I, j, u, or v.*

Build the word *argue*.

"This word is *argue*. What sound does the u make in this word?" */ū/.*

"What is the job of Silent E?" *Silent E keeps u from being the last letter in the word.*

Teach the Sounds of /ū/ and /ōō/ Spelled UE

Build the words *continue* and *avenue*.

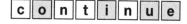 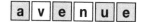

"You already know that long u says /ū/. And you know that sometimes we hear the /y/ part of /ū/ and sometimes we don't."

"Listen to these words: *continue, avenue*. Tell me the sound of the u in each of these words." *In continue, u says /ū/. In avenue, u says /ōō/.*

New Teaching
(continued)

Have your student practice spelling the words *continue* and *avenue*. Point to the u-e in *avenue*. "U-e is usually found at the **end** of words. But we do have one word where it is found in the **middle** of the word."

Build the word *Tuesday*. | t | u | e | s | d | ay |

"When we write out the word *Tuesday* on paper, we capitalize it because it is the name of a day of the week."

Introduce the Word Bank for UE

Have your student read through the **Word Bank for UE** to improve visual memory. There are several ways to spell the sounds of /ū/ and /o͞o/ and we want students to become very familiar with the words in this Word Bank. This will enable the student to choose the correct spelling of /ū/ and /o͞o/ when he needs to spell one of these words.

Teach the Days of the Week

"Tell me the days of the week." *Student responds.*

If your student doesn't know the days of the week in order, take out a calendar and go through them together.

Take out Word Cards 134-140 and spread them out in order.

"Notice that each word ends in *day*. There are a few other things we have to look at, too."

"Take a look at the word *Monday*." Point to the o. "The /ŭ/ sound in *Monday* is spelled with an o. Practice spelling this word." *Student spells the word* Monday.

"The word *Wednesday* is an unusual one. We say /wenz–day/ when we speak, but when we spell the word, we pronounce it for spelling: /wed–nez–day/. Repeat after me: /wed–nez–day/." *Student repeats.*

Step 18: The Sounds of /ū/ and /o͞o/ Spelled UE

New Teaching
(continued)

Take out Word Card 136. "*Wednesday* is a Rule Breaker because it has extra letters that we don't pronounce in normal speech. To remind you to pronounce this word for spelling, underline the three syllables we pronounce for spelling: /wed–nez–day/."

> You'll see that the Rule Breaker receives a different treatment than usual in this lesson.

"Spell the word *Wednesday*." *Student spells the word.*

"*Thursday* is spelled with /er/ as in *nurse*."

"The sound of /ī/ in *Friday* is spelled with the letter i."

"*Saturday* is spelled with /er/ as in *nurse*."

"The *sun* in *Sunday* is spelled like the *sun in the sky*."

Have your student practice spelling the days of the week.

Word Cards 131-140: Spell on Paper

Dictate the words and have your student spell them on paper.

131. argue
132. continue
133. avenue
134. Monday
135. Tuesday
136. Wednesday
137. Thursday
138. Friday
139. Saturday
140. Sunday

File the Word Cards behind the Review divider.

Step 18: The Sounds of /ū/ and /o͞o/ Spelled UE

Reinforcement

Dictate Sentences

Dictate several sentences each day.

The twins were born on Tuesday.
Shall we continue our walk down the avenue?
I didn't catch any shrimp on Friday.
Dan should not argue with his father.
Wednesday comes in the middle of the week.
Mom is wrapping ninety fish in newspaper.
She rewrote the letter two days later.
I was so sleepy Monday morning!
Did the pilgrims go to church on Sunday?
I might go hiking in the woods on Saturday.
Don't you just love surprises?
What would you like to do on Thursday afternoon?

Writing Station

Dictate each word and have your student write it on paper. Then have your student write original sentences using the new words.

wrapped   **eight** (eight basketballs)
presliced   **ate** (ate the hotdogs)
uncooked

Step 19 - PH and the /er/ of *Early*

This lesson will teach words with ph and the sound of /er/ as in early.

You will need: Word Bank for EAR, Word Cards 141-150

Review

Word Bank for UE
Word Bank for ER

New Teaching

Teach Another Way to Spell /er/

"Pull down the tiles that make the sound of /er/." *Student pulls down er, ur, ir, or, and ear.*

Point to the ear tile.

"Today we will work with the ear tile."

"Repeat these words after me and listen for the /er/ sound: *early, earn, heard, search.*" *Student listens and repeats the words.*

"I will dictate some words for you to spell. In each one, the /er/ sound is spelled ear."

Dictate the following words:

   earth   **learn**   **pearl**

Introduce the Word Bank for EAR

Have your student read through the **Word Bank for EAR** to improve visual memory. We want students to become very familiar with the words in this Word Bank before the next spelling for /er/ is introduced.

New Teaching
(continued)

Teach the Sound of /f/ Spelled PH

"Pull down two tiles that say /f/." *Student pulls down f and ph.*

"Most of the time, the sound /f/ is spelled with an f. But some words are spelled with ph. Repeat these words after me and listen for the /f/ sound: *photo, telephone, alphabet, graph.*" *Student listens and repeats the words.*

"These words all have the sound of /f/ spelled ph."

"Build the word *graph* with tiles." *Student builds the word.*

Teach a Rule Breaker

Build the word *minute*.

"This word is *minute*, as in *one minute. Minute* is a Rule Breaker. Which letter doesn't say the sound we expect it to say?" *The u because it says /ĭ/.*

Take out Word Card 150. "What do we do with Rule Breakers?" *Student circles the u and colors in the circle with yellow pencil.*

"Write the word *minute.*" *Student writes the word.*

> Your student may enjoy learning that this word can also be pronounced /mī–NOOT/, meaning *very small*. Words with the same spelling but different pronunciations are called *homographs*.

Spotlight on Silent E

Build the word *telephone* with tiles.

"Here's another word with the sound of /f/ spelled ph. What is this word?" *Telephone.*

Point to the last e. "What is the job of Silent E in this word?" *To make the o long.*

"Good. Let's look again at today's Rule Breaker, *minute*, which also has a Silent E. What kind of e is it?" *A Handyman E because it doesn't fall into the other categories.*

Step 19: PH and the /er/ of *Early*

New Teaching
(continued)

Word Cards 141-150: Spell on Paper

Dictate the words and have your student spell them on paper.

141. early
142. search
143. learn
144. earn   Did he earn that money?
145. earth
146. heard   I heard a loud noise.
147. pearl
148. telephone
149. graph
150. minute

File the Word Cards behind the Review divider.

Reinforcement

More Words

The following words reinforce the concepts taught in Step 19. Have your student spell them for additional practice.

photo   **photograph**   **alphabet**

Homophone Pairs

Have your student add the following homophone pair to the Homophones List.

heard / herd

Read the following sentences and have your student point to the correct word on the Homophones List.

I heard the great news!
The herd of sheep roamed the hillside.
She heard the bells chime.
The students gathered in a big, noisy herd!

Step 19: PH and the /er/ of *Early*

Reinforcement (continued)

Dictate Sentences

Dictate several sentences each day.

> What did you learn about the earth and stars?
> Don't forget that the early bird catches the worm!
> That telephone rings every minute!
> The little girl only knows half of the alphabet.
> His wife hopes to earn a huge income.
> Smile while I take your photograph.
> I heard you whisper my name.
> Search carefully for the pot of gold.
> My husband gave me a lovely pearl pin.
> The graph shows how many fish are in the sea.
> We filled twenty glasses with milk.
> I'll eat anything but uncooked clams.

Writing Station

Dictate each word and have your student write it on paper. Then have your student write original sentences using the new words.

gracefully	**whales**
larger	**too** (too much rain)
learning	

Step 20 - Unaccented A

This lesson will teach two new phonograms and how to spell multisyllable words containing unaccented a.

You will need: letter tiles ti and oe, Phonogram Cards 64 and 65, Sound Cards 73 and 74, Word Bank for Unaccented A, Word Cards 151-160

Review

Word Bank for EAR
Word Bank for EA (/ĕ/)

New Teaching

Teach New Phonograms TI and OE

"We have two new tiles today."

Point to the ti tile. [ti]

"This tile says **/sh/, tall-letter /sh/**. Repeat after me: /sh/, tall-letter /sh/." *Student repeats.*

Point to the oe tile. [oe]

"This tile says **/ō/, two-letter /ō/ that we may use at the end of English words**. Repeat after me: /ō/, two-letter /ō/ that we **may** use at the end of English words." *Student repeats.*

> If your student is curious about the name "tall-letter /sh/," take out all of the letter tiles that spell the /sh/ sound: sh, ti, ci, and si. Notice that ti is written with the tallest letter.
> To help distinguish between the four ways to spell the sound of /sh/, ti is given the nickname "tall-letter /sh/."

Store the new tiles under the following labels:

The Sound of /sh/	Vowel Teams
ti	oe

Take out Phonogram Cards 64 and 65 and practice them with your student.

Practice Sound Cards 73 and 74 with your student. Dictate the sound and have your student write the phonogram.

File the cards behind the appropriate Review dividers in the Spelling Review Box.

New Teaching
(continued)

Teach Unaccented A

Build the word *about*.

"What does this word say?" *About.*

Point to the a. "Sometimes when the letter a comes at the beginning of a multisyllable word, it doesn't say its sound clearly. It sounds like /ŭ/."

"Repeat these words after me and listen for the /ŭ/ sound: *another, across, agreement.*" *Student listens and repeats the words.*

"Now I'll dictate some words for you to spell. In each of these words, the /ŭ/ sound is spelled with an a."

"*Along.*" *Student spells the word.*

"*Agree.* Use *double e* for the /ē/ sound." *Student spells the word.*

"*Away.* Use *two-letter a* for the /ā/ sound." *Student spells the word.*

> The a is a schwa in the unaccented syllable.
>
> Some students find it easier to learn these words if they "pronounce for spelling." Enunciating the long a, as in /ā-long/, is a good spelling strategy.

Introduce the Word Bank for Unaccented A

Have your student read through the **Word Bank for Unaccented A** to improve visual memory.

Teach a Rule Breaker

Build the word *again*. [a][g][ai][n]

"The word *again* is a Rule Breaker. Which letters don't say the sound we expect them to say?" *The ai because it says /ĕ/.*

Take out Word Card 160. "What do we do with Rule Breakers?" *Student circles the ai and fills in the circle with yellow pencil.*

"Write the word *again*." *Student writes the word.*

New Teaching
(continued)

Spotlight on Silent E

Build the word *above* with tiles.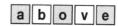

Point to the last <u>e</u>. "What is the job of Silent E in this word?" *To keep the <u>v</u> from being the last letter because English words don't end in <u>v</u>.*

Word Cards 151-160: Spell on Paper

Dictate the words and have your student spell them on paper.

151. about
152. above
153. ago
154. away
155. agree
156. along
157. around
158. amount
159. another
160. again

File the Word Cards behind the Review divider.

Reinforcement

More Words

The following words reinforce the concepts taught in Step 20. Have your student spell them for additional practice.

across   agreement   alike   among
alone

Step 20: Unaccented A

Reinforcement
(continued)

Dictate Sentences

Dictate several sentences each day.

I would like to visit a land far away.
Stamp your feet if you agree with me.
The fox was sniffing around the yard.
Don't drop those trays again!
Your train left about a minute ago.
Their ball rolled across the street.
We rode our bikes along the edge of the pond.
I will vote for another person.
These two dresses look just alike.
Write your names on the agreement.
We'll need a large amount of ink for the copier.
Keep your head above the water!

Writing Station

Dictate each word and have your student write it on paper. Then have your student write original sentences using the new words.

earliest	**worms**
searching	**singing**
trees	

 Is the daily review helping your student internalize all the concepts he's learned so far? Are the decks behind the Mastered dividers getting bigger? Does your student have a firm grasp on the Key Card rules for spelling?

Mastered cards will be reviewed again in Step 23 to keep them fresh in your student's mind.

Step 21 - Long A Spelled EA

In this lesson, your student will learn to spell words containing the sound of /ā/ spelled ea.

You will need: Word Bank for EA (/ā/), Spelling Strategies Chart, Word Cards 161-170

Review

Word Bank for Unaccented A
Word Bank for UE

New Teaching

Teach the Sound of /ā/ Spelled EA

"Repeat these words after me and listen for the /ā/ sound: *great, wear, steak.*" *Student listens and repeats the words.*

"I will dictate some words for you to spell. In each one, the /ā/ sound is spelled *ea*."

Dictate the following words:
- **break** (Did the cat break the vase?)
- **wear** (Wear a hat and gloves!)
- **great** (She's a great person.)
- **bear** (There's a brown bear in the yard!)
- **steak** (I ate a steak for dinner.)

Introduce the Word Bank for EA (/ā/)

Have your student read through the **Word Bank for EA (/ā/)** to improve visual memory. There are several ways to spell the sound of /ā/ and we want students to become very familiar with the words in this Word Bank. This will enable the student to choose the correct spelling of /ā/ when he needs to spell one of these words.

Step 21: Long A Spelled EA

New Teaching
(continued)

Practice Spelling Strategies #1, #2, and #3

Take out Word Cards 166-170 and the Spelling Strategies Chart. Have your student study the words and use whichever spelling strategies are helpful to him. Focus on the first three strategies: Pronounce for Spelling, Analyze the Word, and Scratch Paper Spelling.

fact (Hint: For the /k/ sound, we always try c first.)
next (Hint: We use x for the /ks/ sound.)
between (Hint: Double e is used for the /ē/ sound.)
ground (Hint: We use ou for the /ow/ sound.)
horse (Hint: The Silent E is a Handyman E.)

Word Cards 161-170: Spell on Paper

Dictate the words and have your student spell them on paper.

161. bear A grizzly bear stole our food.
162. great What a great movie!
163. wear Did you wear a hat?
164. break Let's take a break for lunch.
165. steak Dad ate steak and eggs.
166. fact
167. next
168. between
169. ground
170. horse She named her horse Star.

File the Word Cards behind the Review divider.

Reinforcement

More Words

The following words reinforce the concepts taught in Step 21. Have your student spell them for additional practice.

spring   **struck**   **decide**   **act**

Step 21: Long A Spelled EA

Reinforcement
(continued)

Homophone Pairs

Have your student add the following homophone pairs to the Homophones List.

    wear / where   break / brake

Read the following sentences and have your student point to the correct word on the Homophones List.

> **Where** are your goats?
> Use the **brake** on your bike when you go downhill.
> I didn't **break** the lamp!
> She didn't know what to **wear** to the dance.

Dictate Sentences

Dictate several sentences each day.

> Do you prefer steak or fish?
> My brother tells great jokes!
> Decide which helmet you want to wear.
> The knight rode a white horse.
> Cover the ground with seeds.
> That bear ate all of our hotdogs!
> Crush the grapes between your teeth.
> Who is the next person in line?
> Corn grows in the spring.
> It is a fact that foxes have four legs.
> I wish he would act his age!
> Can we take a break now?

Writing Station

Dictate each word and have your student write it on paper. Then have your student write original sentences using the new words.

charging   **knights** (knights in armor)
coming   **riding**
horses

Step 21: Long A Spelled EA

Step 22 - /shŭn/ Spelled TION

In this lesson, your student will learn the most common way to spell the word ending /shŭn/.

You will need: Spelling Strategies Chart, Word Bank for TION, Word Cards 171-180

Review

Word Bank for EAR
Word Bank for EA (/ā/)

New Teaching

Teach the Most Common Way to Spell /shŭn/

"Repeat these words after me and listen for the /shŭn/ sound: *action, motion, question, attention.*" *Student listens and repeats the words.*

"In each of these words, the /shŭn/ sound is spelled ti-o-n."

Pull down the letter tiles. | ti | o | n |

"The syllable /shŭn/ is used in many words. Let's look at a few."

Build the word *action*. | a | c | ti | o | n |

"This word says...?" *Action.*

"Divide this word into syllables." *Student divides between the c and the t.*

"Good. The ti-o-n always stays together in the same syllable."

Build the word *invite*. | i | n | v | i | t | e |

"To change *invite* to *invitation*, we drop the e and add a-ti-o-n."

| i | n | v | i | t | a | ti | o | n |

Step 22: /shŭn/ Spelled TION

New Teaching
(continued)

Discuss Spelling Strategy #4

Build the word *addition*. | a | d | d | i | ti | o | n |

"Do you see a smaller word within the word *addition*?" *Add.*

"*Add* is the base word for *addition*. Knowing the base word can help you spell the word *addition*."

Build the word *information*. | i | n | f | or | m | a | ti | o | n |

"Can you find the base word in *information*?" *Inform.*

"Good. Knowing that the base word is *inform* helps us spell the word correctly."

Uncover Strategy #4 on the Spelling Strategies Chart. "This is Spelling Strategy #4: Identify the Base Word."

"Many words ending in the sound of /shŭn/ have a base word, but not all. For example, the word *motion* doesn't have a base word."

Build the word *motion*. | m | o | ti | o | n |

Introduce the Word Bank for TION

Have your student read through the **Word Bank for TION** to improve visual memory. There are several ways to spell /shŭn/ and we want students to become very familiar with the words in this Word Bank. This will enable the student to choose the correct spelling of /shŭn/ when he needs to spell one of these words.

> Phonogram *ti* is most commonly found in the syllable *tion*. Other syllables that contain *ti*, such as *partial*, *cautious*, and *quotient*, will be taught in later levels.
>
> Likewise, the most common way to spell /shŭn/ is *tion*. Two other ways will be taught in Level 5: *sion* as in *mansion* and *cion* as in *suspicion*.

Step 22: /shŭn/ Spelled TION

New Teaching
(continued)

Word Cards 171-180: Spell on Paper

Dictate the words and have your student spell them on paper.

171. question
172. motion
173. addition
174. action
175. direction
176. information
177. vacation
178. fiction
179. attention
180. mention

File the Word Cards behind the Review divider.

Reinforcement

More Words

The following words reinforce the concepts taught in Step 22. Have your student spell them for additional practice.

condition	station	population	invitation
combination			

Step 22: /shŭn/ Spelled TION

Reinforcement
(continued)

Dictate Sentences

Dictate several sentences each day.

    The action began when the bell rang.
    Did I mention that I earn great grades?
    Please reply to the question.
    The motion of the ship made me ill.
    Nothing is better than summer vacation!
    They skipped joyfully in my direction.
    Are you paying attention to his speech?
    The woman rose gracefully from the stone bench.
    Did you learn addition yet?
    My friends love to read fiction.
    We must ask for more information.
    I sent you an invitation to my party.

Writing Station

Dictate each word and have your student write it on paper. Then have your student write original sentences using the new words.

facts	**bears** (brown bears)
learned	**read** (past tense)
weight (gain weight)	

Step 23 - Ways to Spell /er/

In this lesson, your student will analyze five ways to spell the sound of /er/.

You will need: Sound Card 75

Review

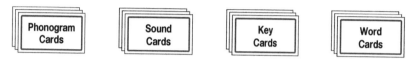

Word Bank for ER
Word Bank for TION

 Quickly review the cards behind the Mastered dividers.

New Teaching

Introduce the Word Sort for /er/

Write these five headings across the top of lined paper. Draw vertical lines to form five columns:

er	ur	ir	or	ear

Point to the column headings. "Here are five ways to spell the sound of /er/."

Give your student a new sheet of lined paper. "I will dictate a word and you will write it down on your paper. When you are satisfied that you have spelled the word correctly, copy the word to the correct column on this chart."

Dictate the following words:

world	earliest	thirty	prefer	birthday
different	worry	purple	skirt	learning
worship	search	serve	heard	curve
return	worker	player	circle	disturb

Step 23: Ways to Spell /er/   117

New Teaching
(continued)

Teach Sound Card 75

"Today we have a new Sound Card."

Read Sound Card 75:

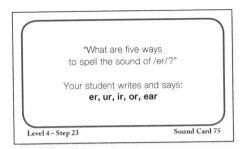

> Now that your student has learned two more ways to spell /er/, Sound Card 58 from Level 3 should be removed from the Spelling Review Box and replaced with Sound Card 75.

"Write and say the five ways like this." Say the names of the letters as you write them down: "er, ur, ir, or, and ear."

Practice this Sound Card with your student and then store it behind the Review divider.

Reinforcement

Dictate Sentences

Dictate several sentences each day.

> There are no new Word Cards for Step 23.

Are you learning all of the facts?
Nineteen bears hid among the trees.
Have you been to the new bus station?
Put a larger photo in the frame.
Do you know the combination to the safe?
My earliest class begins at noon.
Bob put presliced ham on his bread.
My city has a population of only two hundred!
What are you searching for?
Which homes are in the worst condition?
Are you coming over later?
I like riding their ponies.

Reinforcement
(continued)

Writing Station

Dictate each word and have your student write it on paper. Then have your student write original sentences using the new words.

earned **fixing**
telephones **minutes**
worked

Step 24 - /wōr/ Spelled WAR

In this lesson, your student will learn how to spell words containing the pattern war.

You will need: Word Cards 181-190

Review

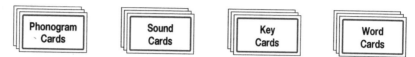

Word Bank for EA (/ā/)
Word Bank for Unaccented A

New Teaching

Teach /wōr/ Spelled WAR

"Repeat these words after me and listen for the /wōr/ sound: *warm, forward, warn, reward.*" Student listens and repeats the words.

"In each of these words, the /wōr/ sound is spelled w-ar." Pull down the w and ar letter tiles.

| w | ar |

Point to the w. "After a w, ar usually sounds like /or/."

"I will dictate some words. In each one, the /wōr/ sound is spelled w-ar."

Dictate the following words:

war   **warm**   **backward**   **reward**   **warn**

Spell the word *quart* with letter tiles. | qu | ar | t |

Point to the qu. "The word *quart* has a /kw/ sound at the beginning. Do you hear the /w/?"

"Even though it doesn't have a w in it, it has the /w/ sound. The sound of the ar tile is changed by the /w/ sound."

"Use the /er/ of *her* to change *quart* to *quarter*."

Step 24: /wōr/ Spelled WAR

New Teaching
(continued)

Teach Two Rule Breakers

"Two words on today's word list are Rule Breakers."

Build the word *hour*. [h][ou][r]

"This word is *hour*. Which letter doesn't say the sound we expect it to say?" *The h because it is silent.*

Show Word Card 189 to your student.

"Circle the h in this word, because it doesn't make the sound we expect it to make." *Student circles the letter and fills in the circle with yellow pencil.*

"Spell the word *hour* on paper." *Student writes the word.*

Build the word *people*. [p][e][o][p][l][e]

"This word is *people*. Just like the word *hour*, this word contains a silent letter. Which letter is silent?" *The o.*

Take out Word Card 190. "Right. Circle the o because it doesn't make the sound we expect it to make." *Student circles the letter and fills in the circle with yellow pencil.*

"Spell the word *people* on paper." *Student writes the word.*

Have your student practice these two words until they become easy.

Spotlight on Silent E

"Look at the word *people* that you just wrote on your paper. It ends in Silent E. What is the job of Silent E in this word?" *It adds a vowel to the last syllable.*

New Teaching
(continued)

Word Cards 181-190: Spell on Paper

Dictate the words and have your student spell them on paper.

    181. warm
    182. war   The war is over.
    183. warn   Did you warn her not to go?
    184. quart
    185. quarter
    186. forward
    187. backward
    188. reward
    189. hour   Stay here for one hour.
    190. people

File the Word Cards behind the Review divider.

Reinforcement

Homophone Pairs

Have your student add the following homophone pair to the Homophones List.

    hour / our

Read the following sentences and have your student point to the correct word on the Homophones List.

    Don't lose <u>our</u> tickets to the game!
    We have to be there in an <u>hour</u>.
    The teacher gave us one <u>hour</u> for the test.
    We'll get <u>our</u> grades tomorrow.

Step 24: /wōr/ Spelled WAR

Reinforcement
(continued)

Dictate Sentences

Dictate several sentences each day.

> Sometimes it is warm even in January.
> There is only a quart of gas in the car.
> Isn't it better to face forward when you ski?
> Sixteen people are judging the contests.
> You have only one hour to finish sketching.
> Why did you walk home backward?
> How much cash have you earned?
> My father did not fight in the war.
> We must warn the other people about the quicksand.
> Did you give your brother a quarter?
> Uncle Ted only worked for forty minutes.
> You will get a reward for your hard work.

Writing Station

Dictate each word and have your student write it on paper. Then have your student write original sentences using the new words.

recheck   **turned**
directions   **way** (way to go)
swiftly

Step 25 - The Sound of /ē/ Spelled EY

In this lesson, your student will learn how to spell words with the sound of /ē/ spelled ey.

You will need: Word Bank for EY (/ē/), Spelling Strategies Chart, Word Cards 191-200

Review

Word Bank for UE
Word Bank for EAR

New Teaching

Teach the Sound of /ē/ Spelled EY

"Repeat these words after me and listen for the /ē/ sound: *money, valley, turkey*." *Student listens and repeats the words.*

"In each of these words, the sound of /ē/ is spelled ey." Pull down the ey letter tile.

ey

> Phonogram ey was first introduced in Level 3.
>
> There are only about forty words that end in ey. The most common ones are taught in this lesson.

"Ey is used only at the end of words."

"I will dictate some words for you to spell. In each one, the /ē/ sound is spelled with ey."

Dictate the following words:

key   **valley**   **chimney**   **turkey**

"In these next words, the /ŭ/ sound is spelled with an o."

money   **monkey**   **honey**

Introduce the Word Bank for EY (/ē/)

Have your student read through the **Word Bank for EY (/ē/)** to improve visual memory. There are several ways to spell the sound of /ē/ and we want students to become very familiar with the words in this Word Bank. This will enable the student to choose the correct spelling of /ē/ when he needs to spell one of these words.

New Teaching
(continued)

Practice Spelling Strategies #1, #2, and #3

Take out Word Cards 198-200 and the Spelling Strategies Chart. With your student, discuss spelling strategies that will help him spell the words. Some words may require the Pronounce for Spelling strategy, and others may require the Analyze the Word or Scratch Paper Spelling strategies.

Word Cards 191-200: Spell on Paper

Dictate the words and have your student spell them on paper.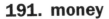

191. money
192. key
193. monkey
194. honey
195. turkey
196. valley
197. chimney
198. because
199. paid
200. inside

File the Word Cards behind the Review divider.

Reinforcement

More Words

The following words reinforce the concepts taught in Step 25. Have your student spell them for additional practice.

cause　　　　**repaid**

Step 25: The Sound of /ē/ Spelled EY

Reinforcement
(continued)

Dictate Sentences

Dictate several sentences each day.

> The monkey yawned and stretched his arms.
> Have you paid for the overdue books?
> They want turkey instead of steak.
> We live in a sunny valley near the sea.
> They never ask for directions!
> Hide your key under the mat on the porch.
> I don't have any money because I spent it all!
> This brick chimney is spotless!
> The bears stole the honey from the hive.
> What is the cause of his sickness?
> The spy slipped inside the black van.
> I spent all day fixing the telephones.

Writing Station

Dictate each word and have your student write it on paper. Then have your student write original sentences using the new words.

- **ungraceful**
- **enjoying**
- **unhinged**
- **turkeys**
- **harmless**

Step 25: The Sound of /ē/ Spelled EY

Step 26 - The Sound of /ō/ Spelled OE

In this lesson, your student will learn how to spell words with the sound of /ō/ spelled oe, and more words with Silent E.

You will need: Word Cards 201-210

Review

Word Bank for EY (/ē/)

New Teaching

Teach the Sound of /ō/ Spelled OE

"Repeat these words after me and listen for the /ō/ sound: *goes, hoe* like the garden tool, *toe* on your foot." *Student listens and repeats the words.*

"In each of these words, the /ō/ sound is spelled oe." Pull down the oe letter tile.

`oe`

"I will dictate some words for you to spell. In each one, spell the /ō/ sound with oe."

Dictate the following words:

hoe (garden tool)   **toe** (on your foot)   **goes**

The list of words with /ō/ spelled oe is very short: *doe, foe, Joe, oboe, roe, throes, woe*, plus the three words taught in this lesson.

New Teaching (continued)

Spotlight on Silent E

Take out Word Cards 201-210. "Each of these words has a Silent E. See if you can determine the job of Silent E."

Word	Student response
before	*Silent E makes the o long.*
close	*Silent E makes the o long.*
unable	*Silent E adds a vowel to the last syllable.*
leave	*Silent E keeps v from being the last letter.*
else	*Silent E is a Handyman E and keeps* else *from looking like a plural word.*
include	*Silent E makes the u long.*
provide	*Silent E makes the i long.*

"Paying attention to the job of Silent E will help you remember how to spell the word."

Word Cards 201-210: Spell on Paper

Dictate the words and have your student spell them on paper.

201. hoe — Did you use the hoe in the garden?
202. toe — She broke her toe.
203. goes
204. before
205. close — Close the door.
206. unable
207. leave
208. else
209. include
210. provide

File the Word Cards behind the Review divider.

Reinforcement   **Dictate Sentences**

Dictate several sentences each day.

The knights would not leave us out here alone!
My toe struck the edge of a rock.
This type of germ is harmless.
He was unable to provide more facts about the case.
Put the hoe back in the shed.
Include your phone number on your test.
We are enjoying this pretty Sunday morning.
Would you say that turkeys are ungraceful birds?
The wheel goes around eighty times an hour.
I stood up and unhinged the cages.
Should we add something else to the shopping list?
Close the gate before the monkey gets out!

Writing Station

Dictate each word and have your student write it on paper. Then have your student write original sentences using the new words.

monkeys   **toes** (on your toes)
stretching   **knees**
hanging

Step 27 - The /ĭk/ Words

In this lesson, your student will learn how to spell words with the common word ending of ic.

You will need: Word Bank for IC, Word Cards 211-220

Review

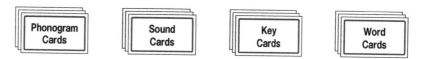

Review All Word Banks

Review the cards behind the Mastered dividers. This is the last review for Level 4, so make it thorough!

New Teaching

Teach the /ĭk/ Words

"Repeat these words after me and pay special attention to the **last syllable**: *fabric, plastic, magic.*" *Student listens and repeats the words.*

"What was the last syllable in each word?" */ĭk/.*

"Right. And at the end of a word, we spell /ĭk/ with i-c." Pull down letter tiles i and c.

"Here are some more words that end in /ĭk/." Build the words *attic* and *music*.

| a | t | t | i | c | | m | u | s | i | c |

"We call these the /ĭk/ *words* because the last part of the word says /ĭk/."

This is a special group of words. Most of the time, when the /k/ sound comes right after a short vowel, it is spelled with ck. In multisyllable words ending in the sound /ĭk/, however, the /k/ sound is spelled with a c.

Step 27: The /ĭk/ Words

New Teaching
(continued)

Introduce the Word Bank for IC

Have your student read through the **Word Bank for IC** to improve visual memory. There are several ways to spell the sound of /k/ and we want students to become very familiar with the words in this Word Bank. This will enable the student to choose the correct spelling of /k/ when he needs to spell one of these words.

Teach a Rule Breaker

Build the word *does*.

"The word *does* is a Rule Breaker. Which letters don't say the sound we expect them to say?" *The oe because they say /ŭ/ instead of /ō/.*

Take out Word Card 220. "What do we do with Rule Breakers?" *Student circles the oe and colors in the circle with yellow pencil.*

"Write the word *does*." *Student writes the word.*

Word Cards 211-220: Spell on Paper

Dictate the words and have your student spell them on paper.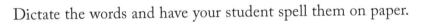

211. music
212. public
213. magic
214. traffic
215. plastic
216. attic
217. fabric
218. topic
219. elastic
220. does

File the Word Cards behind the Review divider.

Step 27: The /ĭk/ Words

Reinforcement

More Words

The following words reinforce the concepts taught in Step 27. Have your student spell them for additional practice.

    electric   **garlic**   **basic**

Dictate Sentences

Dictate several ssentences each day.

- My mother has hundreds of photographs in the attic.
- This park is not open to the public.
- What kind of music do you prefer?
- Stitch the elastic onto the fabric.
- Do you know any magic tricks?
- There was a line of traffic ten miles long.
- Our plastic toys are covered with dirt.
- Which topic are you writing about?
- The electric light does not work.
- Sometimes I find great joy in the most basic things!
- Garlic is a smelly but healthy addition to your cooking.
- Does the teacher mind if I leave early?

Writing Station

Dictate each word and have your student write it on paper. Then have your student write original sentences using the new words.

    gates   **closed**
    locks   **combinations**
    keys

Step 27: The /ĭk/ Words

Celebrate! **Present Your Student with the Certificate of Achievement**

3
Appendices

APPENDIX A
Phonograms Taught in Level 4

Phonograms are letters or letter combinations that represent a single sound. For example, the letter <u>b</u> represents the sound /b/ as in *bat*. The letter combination <u>sh</u> represents the sound /sh/ as in *ship*.

Card #	Phonogram	Sound	For the Teacher's Use Only (example of word containing the phonogram)	Step
54	tch	/ch/, three-letter /ch/	watch	Step 1
55	dge	/j/, three-letter /j/	badge	
56	ew	/o͞o/–/ū/	grew　few	Step 5
57	ei	/ā/–/ē/ that we **may not** use at the end of English words	vein　ceiling	
58	wr	/r/, two-letter /r/ used only at the beginning of a word	write	
59	kn	/n/, two-letter /n/ used only at the beginning of a word	know	
60	or	/or/–/er/ as in *works*	corn　works	Step 7
61	eigh	/ā/, four-letter /ā/	eight	Step 15
62	ear	/er/ as in *early*	early	
63	ph	/f/, two-letter /f/	phrase	
64	ti	/sh/, tall-letter /sh/	nation	Step 20
65	oe	/ō/, two-letter /ō/ that we **may** use at the end of English words	toe	

Appendix A: Phonograms Taught in Level 4

APPENDIX B
Scope and Sequence of Level 4

Your student will:	Step
Review concepts taught in previous levels	1
Learn phonograms tch, dge, and wor	1
Learn when to use ch and when to use tch for /ch/	2
Spell words with the sound of /ch/ spelled ch and tch	2
Learn when to use g and dge to spell /j/ at the end of a word	3
Spell words with the sound of /j/ spelled g and dge	3
Analyze three ways to spell the sound of /j/	4
Learn phonograms ew, ei, wr, and kn	5
Learn how to add prefixes	5
Spell words with prefixes	5
Categorize the four sounds of the letter y	6
Spell words with the different sounds of y	6
Learn another way to spell /er/	7
Spell words with the sound of /wer/ spelled wor	7
Learn to spell the months of the year and common abbreviations	8
Spell words with the sound of /ōō/ spelled ew	9
Learn another way to spell /ĕ/	10
Spell words with the sound of /ĕ/ spelled ea	10
Analyze two ways to spell the sound of /ĕ/	11
Discuss a new spelling strategy	11
Spell words with the sound of /r/ spelled wr	12
Spell words with the sound of /n/ spelled kn	13
Learn more words containing er	14
Learn phonograms eigh, ear, and ph	15
Spell words with the sound of /ŭ/ spelled o	15
Apply spelling strategies to multisyllable words	16
Learn to spell numbers up to one hundred	17
Spell words with the sound of /ā/ spelled eigh	17
Learn to spell the days of the week	18
Spell words with the sounds of /ū/ and /ōō/ spelled ue	18
Learn another way to spell /er/	19
Spell words with /f/ spelled ph and the sound of /er/ spelled ear	19
Learn phonograms ti and oe	20
Spell words containing unaccented a	20
Spell words with the sound of /ā/ spelled ea	21
Learn the most common way to spell the word ending /shŭn/	22
Discuss a new spelling strategy	22
Spell words with the sound of /shŭn/ spelled tion	22
Analyze five ways to spell the sound of /er/	23
Spell words containing the sound of /wōr/ spelled war	24
Spell words with the sound of /ē/ spelled ey	25
Spell words with the sound of /ō/ spelled oe	26
Spell words with the common word ending ic	27

APPENDIX C
The Jobs of Silent E

Depending upon the word in which it is used, Silent E can perform different jobs. These jobs were introduced in Level 2 and Level 3. Use the following graph to refresh your student's memory about the jobs of Silent E.

1	Silent E makes the vowel before it long. n o t e
2	Silent E can make c and g soft. r a c e p a g e
3	Silent E keeps u and v from being the last letter in a word. c l u e g i v e
4	Silent E adds a vowel to a C+le syllable. h a n d l e
5	Handyman E takes care of the jobs the other e's don't cover. • Handyman E keeps a singular word from ending in s. g oo s e • Handyman E is often found in words where the e used to be pronounced. c o m e • Handyman E is added to distinguish between two words. or or e

APPENDIX D
The Six Syllable Types

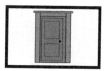 **Closed syllables** are represented by a closed door. In a closed syllable, the vowel is closed in by (that is, followed by) a consonant. In a closed syllable, the vowel is usually short. Examples of closed syllables include *bat, fish,* and *thim–*.

 **Open syllables** are represented by an open door. In an open syllable, the vowel is open; it is the last letter of the syllable and is usually long. Examples include *we, no,* and *ma–*.

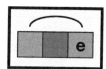 **Vowel-Consonant-E syllables** are represented by three letter tiles: a vowel, a consonant, and an e. The line from the e to the vowel signifies the silent e making the vowel before it long. Examples of this syllable type include *name, hope,* and *–ite*. In the lesson plans, Vowel-Consonant-E is often abbreviated as VCE.

 **Vowel Team syllables** are represented by a team of horses. Just as a team of horses works together, the two vowels in a Vowel Team syllable work together to make one sound. Examples of Vowel Team syllables include *toy, slow,* and *eat*.

 **R-controlled syllables** are represented by Cowboy R roping in the vowels. In this syllable type, the letter r controls the sound of the vowel before it, as in the phonograms <u>or</u>, <u>ar</u>, <u>er</u>, <u>ur</u>, <u>ir</u>, <u>ear</u>, and <u>our</u>. Examples of R-controlled syllables include *her, corn,* and *spar–*.

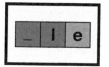 **C+le syllables** are represented by three letter tiles: a consonant, the letter l, and an e. Examples of C+le syllables include *–ble, –ple,* and *–tle*.

APPENDIX E
Words Taught in Level 4

The number listed corresponds with the Step in which the word is first introduced.

A
about 20
above 20
across 20
act 21
action 22
addition 22
afternoon 12
again 20
ago 20
agree 20
agreement 20
alike 20
alone 20
along 20
alphabet 19
among 20
amount 20
another 20
anything 12
anyway 12
Apr. 8
argue 18
armful 14
around 20
attention 22
attic 27
Aug. 8
avenue 18
away 20

B
backward 24
badge 3
basic 27
bear 21
bears 22
because 25
become 15
before 26
begging 2
bench 2
better 14
between 21
blew 9
branch 2
branches 4
bread 10
break 21
bridge 3
bridges 8
brother 15
brownish 2
bunch 2
busier 13
busy 7

C
catch 2
catching 3
cause 25
charge 3
charging 21
chew 9
chewing 12
chimney 25
chopping 4
clipped 14
close 26
closed 27
combination 22
combinations 27
coming 21
complete 16
condition 22
contests 5
continue 18
could 3
cover 15
crunch 2
cutest 15

D
dead 10
deaf 10
Dec. 8
December 8
decide 21
destroy 9
dew 9
die 10
different 16
direction 22
directions 24
ditch 2
does 27
done 15
dozen 15
drew 9

E
earliest 20
early 19
earn 19
earned 23
earth 19
easily 10
easy 6
edge 3
edges 8
eight 17
eighteen 17
eighty 17
elastic 27
electric 27
eleven 17
else 26
enjoying 25
every 6
everything 6
eye 8
eyes 15

F
fabric 27
fact 21
facts 22
family 6
father 14
Feb. 8
February 8
fetch 2
few 9
fiction 22
fixing 23
flew 9
flowers 14
forty 17
forty-four 17
forward 24
fourteen 17
French 2
Friday 18
friend 14
friendly 16
front 15
fudge 3

G
garlic 27
gates 27
goes 26
gracefully 19
graph 19
grassy 14
great 21
grew 9
ground 21
gym 6

H
half 7
hanging 26
harmless 25
head 10
health 10
healthy 10
heard 19
hedge 3
hedges 14
hikes 4
hilltops 12
history 6
hoe 26
honey 25
horse 21
horses 21
hour 24
however 14
hundred 17
husband 16

I
important 16
inch 2
include 26
income 15
information 22
inside 25
instead 10
interest 16
invitation 22
itch 2
itches 3

J
Jan. 8
January 8
judge 3
judging 5
July 8

K
key 25
keys 27
kitchen 2
knee 13
kneel 13
knees 26
knew 13
knife 13
knight 13
knights 21
knit 13
knock 13
knot 13
know 13
known 13

L
larger 19
lead (metal) 10
learn 19
learned 22
learning 19
leave 26
ledge 3
letter 14

Appendix E: Words Taught in Level 4

letters 16
lie 10
lighting 4
locks 27
loudly 2
lunch 2

M
magic 27
Mar. 8
match 2
matter 14
mention 22
minute 19
minutes 23
misprint 5
mistrust 5
Monday 18
money 25
monkey 25
monkeys 26
month 15
mother 15
motion 22
Mr. 8
Mrs. 8
munch 2
munching 15
music 27
myth 6
myths 6

N
neighbor 17
new 9
newest 9
news 9
newspaper 9
next 21
nineteen 17
ninety 17
nonmelting 5
nothing 15
Nov. 8
November 8

O
Oct. 8
October 8
offer 14
other 15
overdo 5
overdue 5
overfilling 11
oversee 5

P
paid 25
patch 2
pearl 19
people 24
person 15

photo 19
photograph 19
pie 10
pies 10
pinch 2
plastic 27
population 22
porch 2
power 14
prefer 14
preheat 11
premade 10
preorder 5
preplan 5
preplanning 5
presliced 18
pretty 6
prizes 9
provide 26
public 27
pulling 5
punch 2

Q
quart 24
quarter 24
question 22

R
races 9
rage 3
ranch 2
reaching 17
read (past tense) 10
ready 10
recheck 24
refer 14
remember 16
rename 5
repaid 25
replies 7
reply 6
reread (present tense) . . . 6
reread (past tense) 16
resold 5
rethink 5
retry 5
revote 5
reward 24
rewrote 16
ridge 3
riding 21
ripping 17
roads 8

S
Saturday 18
says 13
scratch 2
scratching 2
screw 9
search 19

searching 20
second 15
semicircle 5
semiweekly 5
Sept. 8
September 8
serve 14
seventeen 17
seventy 17
should 3
sickness 3
singing 20
sixteen 17
sketch 2
sketched 12
slowly 11
sniffing 15
something 12
sometimes 12
speech 2
spread 10
spring 21
station 22
steak 21
stew 9
stitch 2
stories 6
story 6
stretch 2
stretching 26
struck 21
study 6
studying 6
summer 14
Sunday 18
sunniest 13
sure 13
surprise 16
surprises 17
swiftly 24
switch 2

T
talk 7
telephone 19
telephones 23
thawing 11
their 9
threw 9
Thursday 18
tie 10
toe 26
toes 26
together 16
topic 27
traffic 27
trees 20
Tuesday 18
turkey 25
turkeys 25
turned 24
twenty 17

twenty-eight 17
type 6
typing 7

U
unable 26
uncooked 18
understand 12
unending 5
uneventful 5
ungraceful 25
unhappy 5
unharmful 5
unhinged 25
unlucky 5
unpack 5
unripe 5

V
vacation 22
valley 25

W
walk 7
walking 8
war 24
warm 24
warn 24
wear 21
weather 10
Wednesday 18
weigh 17
weight 17
whales 19
woman 16
women 16
word 7
words 7
work 7
worked 23
worker 13
working 8
world 7
worm 7
worms 20
worry 7
worst 7
worth 7
would 3
wrap 12
wrapped 18
wrapping 17
wrench 12
wrist 12
write 12
wrong 12
wrote 12

Y
yesterday 6

-NOTES-

–NOTES–

-NOTES-

–NOTES–

–NOTES–

–NOTES–

-NOTES-